What to do When
- Gardening reminders monthly, for each part of your garden

Bob Flowerdew

To James

Bob Flowerdew

What to do When
- Gardening reminders monthly, for each part of your garden

Bob Flowerdew 2018

(Expanded from my original idea included in the Organic Bible published by Kyle Cathie)

I dedicate this book to wise gardeners gone before, thanking them for the knowledge and plants they've handed down to us.

Also available
'REALLY HELP YOUR PLANTS'
Plants and other plants, their good and bad companions and worst weeds -being Volume 1 of 'Plant Companions and Co-lives'
'REALLY HELP BUTTERFLIES'
Plants and Lepidoptera; the caterpillars and thus butterflies these plants support -being Volume 2 of 'Plant Companions and Co-lives'
'REALLY HELP YOUR GARDEN ECOLOGY'
Plants and their co-lives, their associated fauna, insects (other than Lepidoptera), nematodes, bacteria, fungi large & small and viruses
-being Volume 3 'Plant Companions and Co-lives'
'REALLY HELP YOUR CROPS'
Farm, orchard and horticultural crops and their associated flora and fauna including worst weeds -extracts from all 3 volumes of 'Plant Companions and Co-lives'

Contents

Introduction

The gardener's year

The Four Seasons tasks spread over 12 months

Tables of 'to be expected' vegetable yields

Tables of vegetable sowing, planting, transplanting and harvesting dates under cover and in the open ground

Introduction

A stitch in time saves nine. This is true for almost everything and particularly gardening. Many a pest outbreak can initially be squashed between finger and thumb but before very long those eggs hatch and the maggots depart all over the plants where they cannot so easily be found.

Indeed much of the skill and relaxed attitude of 'good old boys' is they're well aware of the timing for each and every operation. They know just how long to let weeds grow before they must hoe, when to sow what or prune this and that. Much of this knowledge comes only with a few years experience.

We learn by making mistakes, by doing the right thing at the wrong time and doing the wrong thing at the right time. Each change giving differing results till we get it right. It doesn't matter as long as we do learn from the experience and so become better.

Basically it's much like learning to drive; initially it's all panic, but soon things make sense and before long you're looking further ahead and all becomes automatic.

Until then you may find it useful to follow this book, my accumulated tips and reminders of what must be done and when.

A good idea- Keep a diary of your missed opportunities'

To 'garden' some simply do whatever happens to most take their notice at any given time, thus important jobs may get missed. And as said too many a time "There's a right time for everything in gardening and usually it was last week, or worse; last month!"

In order not to repetitively fall into such error there is a simple solution; keep a diary of missed opportunities. Whenever you find you have forgotten to do something then to prevent this recurring make a note of it in a spare diary putting each note in the week or month the task ought to be performed. These notes will accumulate over the years into your own personal prompter / aide memoire adjusted to the very crops you grow in your own plot with all it's particular variations.

Of course with a few years more experience your 'diary' should become needed less and less often. Until then as I said you have this book!

The gardeners year

'The round of rounds'

Everything in gardening is cyclical and comes round and round and round again. To make it function well we need to undertake each job in turn, and promptly so.

First we can group tasks into those that need doing really frequently, those that need doing fairly regularly, and those seasonal ones that come round once or so each year.

Then within each group we can put these tasks into some sort of order of urgency. Obviously watering dried out plants in pots really needs to be done before cleaning the gutters or writing a seed order. I arrange tasks according to my personal priorities, of course yours may be different but probably most will fall in much the same order.

'The daily round'

Make a daily inspection tour; going round your whole garden noting, and if necessary writing, a 'to do' list of coming up and most pressing jobs (notes such as 'control pests on x', 'sow such and such', 'potting-ups' or 'pruning due') so these may be planned out at leisure, later.

As you progress around your plot your priority is to simultaneously water whatever is wanting.

And then to harvest whatever is going to go over and be wasted unless collected and sent to the kitchen for immediate consumption, processing or storage.

Also simultaneously collect and dispose of litter, collect up junk, tools, toys etc. and put these away out of sight.

Importantly- if you have a cold-frame, walk in tunnel or greenhouse then you need to make a double round, both morning and evening, depending on the season to open and close the ventilation, and/or check min/max thermometers to ensure automatic heating and cooling is sufficiently effective.

'The weekly routine'

The most vital tasks are those daily ones already referred to, only once these are completed should you even consider starting on weekly tasks, some of which you may already have noted are pressing.

The most important of these is to hit windows for sowing and transplanting –so if any are due then do these NOW as next week will be too late!

Afterwards sharpen your hoe and weed the beds and borders.

Once these are clean clip lawn edges and mow the grass.

Dead head fading flowers unless they're needed for fruit or seed. Tie in anything that's flopping about or trim it off.

Collect suitable materials together for composting and move these to your bin. Finally rake or brush down paths and drives.

Have a break, sit down and plan before starting on the seasonal tasks due which you have carefully noted as pressing such as summer pruning and fruit thinning.

'The seasonal cycle'

As everything in gardening is dictated by the season then along with the regular jobs such as the watering, weeding and grass cutting, there are a variety of activities that come around only once or so each year such as hedge trimming, planting bare rooted trees, summer or winter pruning and the preparations for winter.

These more erratic tasks are often easier to over-look till too late than the more frequent chores. Here I've listed the more important.

Obviously the exact timing varies with locality, site and by the same methods anyway, so please make sensible adjustments for yourself and your locality. Remember most plants have similar requirements in much the same order if not in the same week.

(It is interesting to note that each and every variety, of say apple, flowers in strict sequence with all the others in the same place, there are tables available, and these can help identify unknown varieties. The point is though that this sequence is always precisely the same wherever you go, it only starts and stops earlier or later with the place, and year.)

The Four Seasons over 12 months

A year lasts twelve months with, rather optimistically, four seasons. Each season can be notionally divided into early, mid and late, and so very roughly matched to a month just for convenience. These monthly matches work for me here in East Anglia but will need to be modified for other regions with differing micro climates and conditions.

And of course every year is different with the weather appearing to be more erratic than in the past. Still although the exact timing of tasks may change their order will remain much the same.

Many tasks are noted more than once as these can either be performed in either period, or they're just better repeated, or rather more importantly these are really best not forgotten.

The parts of the garden

I have divided the tasks for each month in to the most relevant parts of the garden, again yours may not fit exactly the same, but you will probably have similar.
 First come the tasks for the ornamental and grassed areas.
Then tasks for your fruit cage and orchard subjects.
Followed by the tasks on the vegetable plot.
Then those for wildlife and stock.
What you can do under cover in a potting or tool shed,
And what needs ordering or buying.
Finally with tasks in your greenhouse, tunnel or cold-frame.

Mid Winter

January is the gardens new beginning, at last we're after the winter solstice, the previous year has been laid to rest, the stores are still full, the pruning (hopefully) completed, and the short days are growing longer again.

OUTDOORS IN YOUR GARDEN

On clear bright days make a health and hygiene check and examine each and every plant in your care for damage and dieback, coral spot, scale insects, over-wintering eggs and so on.
Finish pruning work missed earlier but never touch stone fruits or evergreens except when already damaged by winter storms.
cut out broken branches and storm damage to woody plants.
When ground is workable plant out hardy trees and shrubs that missed autumn planting, likewise move or plant hardy herbaceous plants though best not divide at this time.
After hard frosts re-firm roots of earlier plantings as frost loosens soil (called frost-heave).
Stick canes around valuable prostrate plants (e.g. thymes) and emerging bulbs so you see where not to stand in case it snows.
Spread lime on turf as long as that's not of very fine acid loving grass or where you have any lime haters growing nearby.
Use a daisy grubber to rid turf of over-wintering rosette weeds such as thistles.
Rake bare soil, mulches and gravel to prevent these panning.
Coldest weather usually comes next month, so double check outside taps, pipes, gutters and drains.
Spread sharp sand on mossy/algae/weed infested stepping stones and paving so these wear clean, and are less slippery.

MID WINTER / JANUARY IN YOUR FRUIT CAGE & ORCHARD

If deep snow comes wrap old clothes or wire netting around fruit tree trunks to stop rabbits chewing the bark.

Knock heavy snow off fruit cage roof, valuable plants and anything bending under the weight.
If heavy snows last protect plum and gooseberry buds from bullfinches with nets or bird scarers.
Cover outdoor peach and nectarines with plastic sheet as if kept dry over these next months they do not suffer leaf curl so badly.
Check straps and tree ties are neither tight nor slack and stakes solid.
Set or re-touch anti-crawling-pest sticky bands around tree trunks.
Cut to ground all canes of autumn fruiting raspberries.
Finish most fruit tree and bush pruning though leave stone fruits alone unless already damaged.
On a bright sunny day take a long cane and knock any mummified fruits off trees as this considerably reduces rots later.
Scrape loose bark off old grapevines (after they've been pruned) to remove hidden pests.
Spread garden compost around fruit trees and bushes in a thick doughnut shaped ring so it will break down and weather in slowly.

MID WINTER / JANUARY IN YOUR VEGETABLE PLOT

Spread lime on vegetable beds, ideally in the rotation before the Brassicas or Legumes and long before the potatoes return.
Start digging in ryegrass and tougher green manures so they will have died, broken down and incorporated by the time you want to sow and plant.
Or cover them with opaque geo-textile, the green manure will die and be incorporated by the time the beds are needed.
If the ground gets frozen hard wait till it starts to melt then try hoeing, if there are few stones the melted top layer slices off a treat.
Rake the asparagus bed then sprinkle finely powdered charcoal, soot or fine potting compost (take care not to breathe these in) to darken and warm the soil and give an earlier crop.
Likewise darken soil around garlic, seakale and rhubarb, put a large container full of straw over these last two.
Go on a slug and snail hunt turning over their hibernating haunts.
When severe weather threatens cover winter cabbages and less hardy Brassicas with straw or similar and a plastic sheet.

MID WINTER / JANUARY WILDLIFE & STOCK

Clean out bird boxes so they're parasite free, and put up more as these will be needed very soon if it's a mild winter.
Put out food daily and clean and refill water in bird baths, clean bird feeders.
Put out rat-bait, mouse-bait and traps, yes, yes, yes, I know, but do it!
Make sure there's a breathing hole in pond ice, float a ball to bob.
Right now is good time to buy hens- they'll settle down quickly as they're about to come into lay.
As hens will soon start to lay prepare nest boxes with clean straw.

MID WINTER / JANUARY IN YOUR POTTING SHED

Tidy up the garden shed, go on, you know it needs it.
Check through your stores throwing out rotters before they multiply.
Process or use up any stores that are fading.
Sort your seeds into batches by sowing dates and discard really old packets.
Keep all seeds in sealed box or jar, or better still a dead fridge.
Make bird boxes, slug pubs, insect traps, hibernation quarters and plastic bottle cloches.
Start collecting dead cds and dvds to make bird scarers later in year.
Treat yourself to a file or carborundum stone, or even better a grinding attachment for an electric drill, then sharpen your hoe and all other tools with an edge such as spade and trowels.
Paint your post code in bold letters with bright paint on any new and valuable tools, in several places, some bold some hidden.
Glue plastic bottle caps onto the top of garden canes then you will push these in more easily, these'll keep the water out so the canes will last longer and you'll be less likely to impale yourself.
When did you last lubricate your garden gate and shed door catches and hinges, the wheel on your barrow and those on the mower - they all work easier if you do.
Clean and repair or send off the mower so it will be ready to roll!

MID WINTER / JANUARY ORDER & BUY

Make sure your seed orders go in NOW if not done already!

Not too late to order more trees, soft fruit, shrubs, roses and herbaceous plants for immediate planting (if soil friable) when they arrive, or if frozen 'heel in' (dig trench, insert roots, cover with soil or compost, or 'plant' in plastic bags of loose moist compost).
Buy a some more water butts now before the last winter rains come.
If you haven't an asparagus bed order crowns now for planting in a month or so time, in the meantime dig, enrich and prepare site ready.

MID WINTER / JANUARY IN YOUR GREENHOUSE

Give your greenhouse, cold-frame and cloche glass another good clean.
Use only warm tap water for small plants and early sowings to prevent disease.
Bring bags of sowing compost into warm room to preheat before use.
Remove and replace (all probably) pest infested strings and canes.
Sow onion and leek seed in small pots or trays in warmth.
Sow pak-choi, loose leaf lettuce, spring onions and rocket densely in pots or trays of compost under cover to be cut as salad leaves.
Sow pots of sweet peas and Night Scented stocks for indoor flowering.
It's a tad early but sow Sub-Arctic Plenty tomato seed in warmth.
It's not too early to sow indoor all female disease resisting mini cucumbers in warmth and light- they'll probably crop by Easter!
Start onion, garlic and shallot sets in multi celled trays then later once these have made root-balls they can be more securely planted out and will stay put.
Pot up a washed sweet potato in moist gritty compost in warmth to force shoots for this year's plants.
Plant extra early Early potato sets in big pots, bags or tubs for crops by Easter.
Chit your Early seed potatoes (sets) - stand them rose (lots of eyes) end up in a cool light place, an unheated greenhouse will do if sets covered with a 'duvet' on frosty days and cold nights.
Check your chitting potato shoots for aphids and mealy bugs.
Trap slugs, woodlice and other active pests in hollowed out roots, potatoes or under bits of old wood.

Late Winter

This falls in February most years, often bringing the very worst weather, hardest frosts and heaviest falls of snow, use every mild day wisely. Don't be misled by a warm spell, for sure it will be temporary.

OUTDOORS IN YOUR GARDEN

Check fences, tree straps, ties and stakes after each gale.
Stick canes around emerging bulbs and plants so you can see where not to stand in case of deep snow.
When ground is workable plant out hardy trees and shrubs that missed autumn planting.
After hard frosts re-firm roots of autumn plantings.
Do major pruning work missed earlier but do not touch stone fruits or evergreens unless damaged by winter storms.
Stretch cotton over crocus flowers to thwart the birds.
Mark congested clumps of snowdrops, and other early bulbs, for lifting and dividing after the flowers finish.
Make sure weeds aren't getting away, pull up easily at this time, stinging nettles are easy right now- pull furthest runners first.
Spread loose mulches under and around everything, preferably immediately after a period of heavy rain.
Try hoeing as the top surface melts after a long hard frost- the weeds are held fast and slice off cleanly (Only works in stone free soil or with a hoeing mulch of sand or compost).
Spread sharp sand on mossy/algae/weed infested stepping stones and paving so these wear clean, and are less slippery underfoot.
Over-sow balding and worn spots in grass swards -with a fork make many wee holes first then brush the seed in with a stiff broom.

LATE WINTER / FEBRUARY IN YOUR FRUIT CAGE & ORCHARD

On a bright sunny day take a long cane and knock any remaining mummified fruits off trees as this considerably reduces rots later.

On a bright day look for and prune out self descriptive Coral spot and any huge Big Buds on blackcurrants, remove and burn both of these.
Cover outdoor peach and nectarines with plastic sheet as if kept dry over these months they do not suffer Peach leaf curl disease so much.
Or spray peaches & almonds (and flowering versions) when buds are swelling with Bordeaux mixture against leaf curl (where this still permitted).
Empty fruit tree crawling-pest traps (cloth or cardboard bands wrapped around tree trunks), and renew sticky bands.
Divide clumps of chives into small bunches to under-plant your fruit trees to deter fungal diseases, or line a path with them, they'll fill out real fast.
Spread wood ashes not saved for potato and onion crops around your cooking apples and gooseberries.

LATE WINTER / FEBRUARY IN YOUR VEGETABLE PLOT

Pre-warm the beds where you are going to plant early potatoes with black plastic sheet and/or cloches.
Dig in the tougher green manures so these will have died, broken down and incorporated by the time you want to sow and plant.
If your soil is dryish and not frozen you can plant onion, shallots and garlic sets, best on, in or under slight ridges.
Dust soot or dark compost onto, raked and weeded, asparagus beds for earlier crops, likewise for rhubarb and seakale.
Do watch out for perennial weeds surfacing and remove these.

LATE WINTER / FEBRUARY WILDLIFE & STOCK

Put up more bird boxes a.s.a.p. because small insectivorous friends like wrens and tits build their nests this early in the year.
Clean out pest infested material from old bird nest boxes as these'll be needed again VERY VERY soon.
Hang fat balls and seed feeders over your rose bushes and soft fruit so tits awaiting their turn will clean aphid eggs off these.
Put out old, unviable, but only if untreated, seed for birds.
Don't forget to clean and re-fill birdbath again and again.
Rake mulches and bare soil aside to assist birds looking for snacks especially when it has snowed.

Lay an old carpet on any bare soil or turf, after a week move it aside to reveal loads of grubs and slugs to the birds.
Make sure there's a breathing hole in pond ice, float a ball which will bob.
Set mouse and rat bait- they're always increasing and need control!

LATE WINTER / FEBRUARY IN YOUR POTTING SHED

Check your stores, remove any starting to rot before these infect others.
Convert softening apples to puree or bottle these so not wasted.
Convert softening onions to fried ones then freeze these in well sealed bags or containers to prevent taint.
Make sure all your edged tools such as shears, secateurs, spades and most importantly hoes are frighteningly sharp, oiled and ready.
Why not hire an electric grinder to put a really good edge on your tools, then do your friend / parents tools too.
Sort your seeds into batches of similar sowing time and write out the labels ready to save time later.
Put silica gel or similar 'drying agent' pouches (photographers and electrical spares stores have these) in with your seed packets to keep them drier (re-dry these pouches every so often somewhere arid).

LATE WINTER FEBRUARY ORDER & BUY

Get your new seeds and plants if you've not already, especially onion and potato sets, and any fertilisers you may require.
Buy new bags of sowing compost from dry fast moving stacks.
Is your mower ready? If not then hurry up, take your mower for a service- properly maintained it will consume less energy, both fuel and yours!

LATE WINTER / FEBRUARY IN YOUR GREENHOUSE

Inspect plants under cover and indoors removing dead leaves etc. to prevent grey mould getting a start.
Bring sowing and potting composts into warmth at least a day or more before intending using them.

Paint your watering can, or a plastic water bottle black and stand in sun or close by a radiator to have warmer water for new seedlings.

Place mirrors, aluminum foil or just white paper to reflect more valuable light onto your most important plants under cover.

To save heat at night place an aluminised 'space blanket' (from camping stores) over your propagator, or make your own from empty metallised plastic coffee bags stapled together.

Chit early potato 'seed' on (egg) trays in a light, frost free position.

Start off onion and shallot sets in pots or modules under cover as then they only need planting out once as their root-balls can be firmed in so the worms and birds can't shift them.

Pack washed sweet potato in gritty sowing compost and keep moist and warm to force shoots to pot on.

Sow early half hardy bedding plants in small pots in warmth.

Sow hardy scented annuals such as alyssum and mignonette, thinly, in seed trays full of compost or in big pots, especially Night Scented stocks as their evening perfume is a delight, add some Virginian stocks for daytime prettiness.

Sow early batches of indoor tomatoes, cucumbers, hot and sweet peppers, aubergines and basil in individual pots in warmth.

Sow rocket and most other saladings and leafy salad leaves in multicelled trays or small pots.

Pot on just about everything already growing in the greenhouse or indoors, if you can't pot on top dress with enriched potting compost.

Lift, pot and bring under cover clumps of chives and mint roots to force for earlier pickings.

Bring in tub grown grapevines, peaches, apricots, strawberry and gooseberry plants for forcing under cover for super early crops.

Stand pots of Fuschias, Primulas and other plants prone to vine weevil or slugs in saucers sat within bigger saucers with the gap kept full of water as a moat.

Have a slug, snail and woodlice hunt before they multiply.

Early Spring

This should be March but it's hard to tell, it's from now on the biggest workload arrives with grass and weeds starting into growth, indoors plants begin to motor and almost everything hardy needs sowing and / or needs potting up.

OUTDOORS IN YOUR GARDEN

Examine each and every plant in your care for pests, diseases and dieback before they leaf up and it's harder to inspect them.
Do any leftover pruning NOW before growth resumes and the leaves block your sight.
Prune roses and tender plants, evergreens, perennial herbs and hollow stemmed shrubs such as Bamboos and Buddleijas.
Dead head earlier flowering bulbs to improve their flowering next year, divide those that are congested as their leaves wither.
Weeds start germinating in profusion so hoe early and hoe often, hoe, hoe, hoe and hand weed everywhere every other week at least.
Apply new and extra mulches now to trap winter moisture underneath.
As soon as ground is workable plant out evergreens, herbaceous plants, herbs and roses.
Have a snail hunt turning out their haunts and thin numbers before they breed and multiply.
For a really green lawn, pee in the watering can, dilute well and apply often.
Give your grass the first cut with an old blade not a new one as that first cut has to deal with debris left after winter.
Also to start with set mower blades really high to remove tussock forming grasses before they get stronger, then each time you cut lower the height a tad, and so on.
Cut the grass at least fortnightly at first, preferably weekly, collect the clippings to put around fruit trees and bushes, roses and shrubs. Though once a month cut without the box so as to return clippings to feed the worms who will convert these into fertility.

Move, lay and repair turf now if no hard frosts likely.
Remake / trim edges of turfed areas, put pieces in black plastic bag to rot as this makes excellent addition to potting composts.
Over-sow bare bits of grass with seed and rake this in, use tough recreation seed not fine or fancy unless you need a bowling green.
Sow hardy flowers in situ, then cover seeds with spent potting compost to reduce weeds.
Add a measure of seaweed solution to your watering to provide trace elements for your plants.
Also spray everything in the garden with dilute seaweed solution to act as a tonic.
Cut first leaves of comfrey, borage and stinging nettles to rot into liquid feed to soon give to spring greens and plants in pots.
Although it may be raining plants with large foliage in small pots may stay dry so need watering well as these start growing strongly.
Pull stinging nettles and other weeds as these come back to life.
Nip off stinging nettle tips, with gloves, fry with bacon for tasty treat.

EARLY SPRING / MARCH IN YOUR FRUIT CAGE & ORCHARD

If you still have pruning or training to do do it now, especially check for winter breakages that need cutting out.
Spread wood-ashes around fruit trees and soft fruit, especially the older cooking apples and gooseberries.
Hand pollinate first blossoms with a soft paint brush, or a cotton wool ball, I use a feather duster, as few bees are about so early.
Re-plenish, or make, sticky bands round trunks of fruit trees to stop pests climbing up to attack opening buds.
On a bright day look for huge Big Buds (near spherical and several times bigger than healthy pointed buds) on blackcurrants, remove and burn whole stems with these.
On still cold nights protect blossoms and young fruitlets from frost damage with net curtains or sheets fixed over them.
As soon as your soil is workable plant any remaining fruit trees and bushes.
Check ties, stakes and wires before growth obscures them.
Thin apricot and peach fruitlets on walls as soon as there are any set.
Spread sieved garden compost and organic fertilisers under soft and tree fruit to be washed in by rain.

EARLY SPRING / MARCH IN YOUR VEGETABLE PLOT

Tidy up dead and decaying leaves on over-wintered crops to prevent these re-infecting fresh crops.

As soon as possible plant artichokes, asparagus, seakale and rhubarb crowns.

Set garlic cloves, onion sets, shallots.

Start planting out potato sets once your soil is friable, preferably under cloches, Mains as soon as Earlies as they need the longest time to crop.

When planting your Earlies leave all the shoots on, but rub off all bar three developing on your Main crops, and preferably leave those from the rose end.

When planting Main-crop potatoes sow broad beans with each set as a catch crop, after they finish their root nodules feed the spuds.

Sow outdoors in warm soil, preferably under cloches; peas and broad beans, onions, leeks, beetroot, kohl rabi, cabbages, cauliflowers, lettuce, spinach, turnips, carrots, chards, salsify, scorzonera, parsnips, herbs, radishes, spring onions, sweet peas and hardy annuals.

Sow first carrots by covering seeds with sowing compost not soil to keep down weeds and use fleece to keep off their fly.

When sowing parsley pour boiling water in the drill first to kill weed seeds and warm the soil a bit.

Do not pre-soak early sowings of peas (counter-productive, this is only useful later in a dry season), and sow on flat or a low ridge rather than deep in a cold drill.

Put pea guards or similar protection over all your sowings as birds are active now and scratch up everywhere.

Set slug pubs, saucers of beer or juice, now amongst over-wintering and seedling crops to thin out their numbers before they multiply.

Give areas chosen to grow Brassicas later this year a dressing of lime at a handful per square yard.

Sow borage in empty beds to later pull, and compost or make into liquid feed, when you need the space.

Asparagus, seakale and rhubarb will be cropping soon, cut early and regularly, and to ensure future years crops stop sooner than later.

EARLY SPRING / MARCH WILDLIFE & STOCK

Stop feeding nuts to birds as these may choke chicks, feed bread crusts, and fats, don't forget the bird-bath still needs clean water.
Hang up hair and fibrous material on hedges to help the birds still building nests.
A bowl of mud on or by the bird-table will help those birds needing this for their nests.
Hens will be trying to sit on their eggs very soon, no problem if you want chicks, indeed the earlier the better, however check nests often and remove fresh eggs otherwise (mark the ones left to hatch).
Do not forget your hens will need more lime now as they lay so give them crushed shell, or baked crushed eggshells (never give them unbaked eggshell as this risks disease and egg eating).

EARLY SPRING / MARCH IN YOUR POTTING SHED

Check stores, remove everything starting to rot before these infect others, your hens or birds may still appreciate these..
With remaining stored apples, spuds, onions, carrots and so on- process those looking dubious before they're totally wasted.
Don't forget to top up rodent bait and traps as with a shortage of natural food now's the best time to get them.
Paint your butts and watering cans black outside, they pre-warm water whenever the sun touches them.
Collect used but unreadable labels, wash, dry then sandpaper off redundant writing for re-use.
Write labels indoors a night beforehand and slip in seed packet ready rather than do it out in cold and damp later.
Sieve sowing and potting composts ready for use, this breaks up big lumps but do not sieve too finely as small lumpos aid drainage and aeration. Main reason for sieving though is to re-introduce air!
Spend a lot of time in wellies- why not walk on carpet? Cut in-soles from a nice soft remnant. I walk everywhere on red carpet!

EARLY SPRING / MARCH ORDER & BUY

If it's too late for ordering mail order you can still get most seeds, sets and spring plants at your local garden centre.

Order bulbs and plants for summer bedding, don't have them come too soon as growing without check will be best.
Buy more potting compost than you think you'll need so you end up potting up generously rather than meanly.
Buy a new blade for your mower to fit once first cuts are done.

EARLY SPRING / MARCH IN YOUR GREENHOUSE

Sun can be hot from now on so check greenhouse and coldframe ventilation regularly.
Be very careful not to over-water young or tender plants especially on colder days.
Inspect all plants under cover, even in the propagator, for slugs, woodlice, aphids and other pests before these multiply.
Pollinate early flowering plants under cover by hand.
Bring sowing and potting composts indoors to warm over-night before use.
When sowing try dusting your seeds with flour so you can see them better.
Sow plants in warm for growing on under cover; tomatoes, cucumbers, aubergines, sweet and hot peppers.
Sow quick salad crops in trays for small fresh leaves.
Sow half hardy annual flowering plants in cells or pots to plant out later.
Pot on all seedlings and young plants before they become potbound.
Sow sweet corn from end of month in warm and grow on indoors individually in bucket sized pots for a super-early crop.
Bring in second batch of tubs of grapevines, potted gooseberry bushes and strawberry plants for forcing for more early crops.
Sow the most blight resisting tomatoes such as Ferline at the end of the month in the warm for planting outdoors later.
If you have warmth sow melons for growing on under cover.

Mid Spring

Hopefully this it's a kind warm April with no late frosts, but be prepared. Sunshine and showers. Mow, Mow, Mow, Sow, Sow, Sow, Hoe, Hoe, Hoe, says it all

OUTDOORS IN YOUR GARDEN

Once a week go round with a notepad making lists of things to do.
Make sure no weeds are getting away so now hoe at least weekly.
Cut all grass paths and swards weekly, collect clippings to use as mulch and for hotbeds.
Hand grub plantains and thistles from turf then drop a little grass seed in each hole.
Sprinkling garden lime over weedy rough turf will encourage grass and clover and discourage veronica speedwells and buttercups.
Mark the sites of congested flowering bulbs for moving later (and do so before their leaves fade away).
Don't panic if some plants have not leafed up, last winter's cold may have killed some but many are just dormant and may yet recover.
Feed and top dress or pot up perennial plants in pots, tubs and containers, especially those longest overdue.
Tie in new growths of climbing plants, push canes around herbaceous plants and also tie these up earlier not later.
Deadhead, prune and cut back most early flowering shrubs as soon as their flowers fade.
Almost everything is in bud or leaf now so spray dilute seaweed solution everywhere on everything and more heavily on anything showing deficiency symptoms.
Instead of putting all weeds straight onto the compost heap rot the young lush ones in a bucket of water, full of nitrogen these make a liquid feed good for older tougher perennials.
Go round oiling all hinges, latches, catches, the wheel on your barrow, and anything else that needs lubrication just to make your life smoother.

MID SPRING / APRIL IN YOUR FRUIT CAGE & ORCHARD

De-flower all brand new fruit trees and bushes to give them a chance to establish (some think it permissible to let just one fruit set on each plant so as to be sure you have the right variety).
Hand pollinate most valuable fruits, I use a feather duster.
Protect blossoms and young fruitlets from frost with net curtains, plastic sheet or newspaper.
Tie in new shoots of vines sooner rather than later and after thinning number of shoots (and do not panic, off walls in cold sites vines may not break for another month or more).
Put out pheromone traps for such as codling and plum moths.
Start inspecting gooseberries for tiny holes in one lower leaf, these are sawfly caterpillars and squish them or you will lose all foliage.

MID SPRING / APRIL IN YOUR VEGETABLE PLOT

Plant out potatoes, onion seedlings, sets if you have not already, annual herbs and earliest Brassicas.
When planting potatoes add wood ashes or comfrey leaves to their soil to replace the potassium washed out over winter by the rains.
Start to earth up around potato plants as these show with soil or do same with grass clippings.
Have some old sheets or newspapers handy to rush out and cover those potato shoots on frosty nights.
Thin out young onions, carrots, beets and leeks as crowding causes bolting.
Sow; peas, broad beans, most brassicas, lettuces and saladings, herbs, spinach, turnips, carrots, Swedes, salsify, scorzonera, radishes, kohl rabi, fennel, leeks, parsnips, sweet peas and hardy annuals
Sow sweet corn singly directly in situ for the best plants, on a wee ridge and or ideally under bottle cloches (open ended clear tubes made from plastic bottles - aid watering and earthing up) and sow some more seeds in pots to fill in misses.
Sow clumps of Pot marigolds, Phacelia tanacetiifolia, Buckwheat, and Crimson Clover in little patches to attract beneficial insects through summer.

Make night time inspections, with a torch and an instrument of destruction, for all the usual culprits-especially in the sowing and propagation areas.

Cut old roots and spuds in half, hollow out and lay besides new sowings to trap slugs, and put slug pubs out now as on warmer wet nights they'll be about for sure.

Where you are about to plant out or sow squashes, marrows, courgettes or pumpkins mix loads of fresh grass clippings into the soil as this works wonders for them.

Cover those same spots where you intend to grow those squashes, courgettes or pumpkins with a black plastic sheet to pre-warm the soil and exclude weeds.

Where you are going to plant outdoor tomatoes make a temporary tent come flysheet out of clear plastic sheet to pre-warm the soil and protect them while they establish.

Control asparagus beetle; leave one plant to form fern attracting the beetles to lay their eggs on it, cut that one down and burn it the week you stop cutting all the rest.

Don't forget the old trick of cutting a cross in the stem of spring cabbages as you harvest these to get a bonus of small ones later.

MID SPRING / APRIL WILDLIFE & STOCK

Make a weekly tour looking for nests and on sunny days watch out for ladybirds and the first butterflies.

I collect some of the ladybirds to release in my greenhouse to protect my crops there.

Plant teasels, Alchemilla mollis and lupins as all these retain rain and dew in leafy hollows to refresh birds and insects.

Don't forget the bird-bath as water will evaporate and leave the birds thirsty.

Put a pot of mud on the bird table for arriving summer birds who need it for their nests.

Become a spider sanctuary- collect these from arachnophobic neighbours for your greenhouse as they're all predators and not one harms a plant.

MID SPRING / APRIL IN YOUR POTTING SHED

Use up or process all stored fruits and vegetables as these will not last much longer, clean out stores once empty.
If any seed is thought or proves dubious sow some in a pot and watch results.
Likewise sow some soil in a pot and watch to get to know your commonest weeds from their earliest stages.
Pot up house plants- or top dress if their pots are too big already.
Also don't forget your house plants will now need regular watering again.

MID SPRING / APRIL ORDER & BUY

Rush out for potato and onion sets as these will all soon be gone.
If you are short of any vegetable or bedding plants there's still time to order some for planting now or in the next few weeks.
If you wish for hens to lay this winter buy just hatched chicks now to grow on, likewise for ducklings for eggs and slug and snail control.

MID SPRING / APRIL IN YOUR GREENHOUSE

The sun can get unexpectedly hot this time of year- make sure your greenhouse or cold-frame is really well ventilated so your seedlings don't cook.
Examine each and every plant in your care for early signs of pests and diseases especially white fly, red spider mites, scale insects and mealy bugs.
Make night time inspections to catch the slugs and snails.
Place short pieces of old wooden planks under seed-trays, pots, etc. and then inspect weekly to remove slugs and wood lice congregating there (car vacuum cleaner catches the fast ones).
Having trouble germinating seeds. Every year I buy several sorts of sowing compost and trial these, they vary significantly but all perform better than potting or multipurpose composts.
A mixture of sowing composts usually works better, and it really helps to mix in powdered charcoal to darken, aerate and sweeten.
Sow fast growing tender crops with bottom heat, outdoor tomatoes, courgettes, marrows, ridge cucumbers, gherkins, squashes, pumpkins, melons, watermelons in warm to plant out in a month or so time.

Sow runner, climbing and dwarf French beans in pots to plant out later, mix in some sweet peas with climbers to bring in pollinators.
Soak thirsty plants in trays of water for half hour then drain as this is more effective than watering from the top.
Start to give most plants in pots liquid feed in their water.
Keep potting up young plants regularly and well before they need it as late is too late and gives poor results.
Shade the sunny side of sweet and chilli pepper plant pots to keep their roots cool (honest this is really important).
If weather turns hot for days watch out for red spider mite on plants under cover especially melons and cucumbers- use hand lens to spot the little horrors, then mist, use soft soap and introduce predators. Likewise watch for white fly and follow same advice.
Sow more batches of sweet peas and night scented stocks for summer scent.
Remove most side-shoots from tomato plants to re-direct growth to flowers (I leave 1 or 2 strong side-shoots near base to give double or triple rather than single cordon plants as these are squatter).
Pot up removed tomato shoots as these make even better plants than the originals (never buy six of the same as this trick works so well, the rooted side shoots make shorter squatter plants that have their first trusses much lower).
Likewise root the tips of sweet potato, cucumber and melon plants to get more of these for free.
Buy or sow trays of French marigolds to pot up and plant out in the greenhouse and by the tomatoes to keep the whitefly at bay.
De-head French marigold and other such plants until after you've put them out as then these establish better and are more bushy.

Late Spring

May, often considered the start of summer, be realistic, unless you live in a sheltered warm area it is still spring if not winter! Even so there are long days, everything is in full flush of growth, especially the weeds and grass! And so many plants started inside need moving out but not until the middle or even later this month as there's the danger of late hard frosts, it's your call...

OUTDOORS IN YOUR GARDEN

This month often experiences late hard frosts so have sheets and newspapers ready to lay over newly planted bedding.
Establish a watering round for all pot and tub plants on at least a daily basis (if these require more often than this you probably need to them pot up!)!
Examine each and every plant for pests and diseases regularly.
Weeds germinate and grow like topsy this month so hoe, hoe, hoe; and to make this much easier and more effective put a sharp edge on your hoe every ten minutes or so with a sharpening stone or file.
Spray everything with diluted seaweed solution, and anything with deficiency symptoms more heavily.
Cut grass at the very least fortnightly, preferably weekly, returning clippings or after each cut put these in thin layers around roses, shrubs and fruit trees and bushes- but don't pile against trunks or stems which may cause rot.
Tie in and support climbers and taller herbaceous plants.
Dead head and prune most spring flowering shrubs as these go over, especially lilacs, as seeds rob next years flowers.
Likewise nip off seed heads forming on flowering bulbs before those ripen.
Collect comfrey and borage leaves, trample in a bucket, cover with water and hold down with a brick, to make a liquid feed to dilute and apply in a few weeks time.

LATE SPRING / MAY IN YOUR FRUIT CAGE & ORCHARD

On still cold nights protect the blossoms and young fruitlets from frost damage with sheets or fine netting.

Put jam jars over strawberry flowers to keep off birds and weather.

Save doing much summer pruning later, on trained fruit rub off inappropriate shoots (those over-crowded or heading in wrong direction) whilst these are small, especially thin grapevines as these always need it.

Make daily inspections of gooseberry bushes paying special attention to lower leaves, looking for lots of tiny holes; the first signs of attack of the dreaded sawfly caterpillars which can be squished with finger and thumb or detached with leaf and burnt or buried.

Thin gooseberries really hard this early as the small ones make excellent jams and tarts and the remainder will get much bigger

Thin other early fruits such as apricots and peaches, really hard, be ruthless.

LATE SPRING / MAY IN YOUR VEGETABLE PLOT

This month often experiences late hard frosts so have sheets and newspapers ready to lay over newly planted more tender crops and especially the potatoes and tomatoes.

Pre-warm the sites for outdoor tomatoes, pumpkins and squashes by laying black plastic (or clear, or even woven ground cover fabric) sheeting on ground, hold it down well to stop it blowing away, possibly add another clear plastic sheet held up on sticks to make a temporary cloche.

Although not strictly necessary it really helps potatoes, broad beans and peas to draw soil up around the haulm (stems) as this supports them and encourages bigger yields, earth up potato plants later with grass clippings.

Watch for the flowers appearing on early potato plants and when you see these give a huge watering as this significantly increases their crop.

Go round the potatoes and remove those flowers and seed pods which also will increase the crop.

Sow sweet corn as you can never have too much and plants direct sown in situ right now will often make the best cobs (ripening in late summer).

Sow small batches of turnips for summer crops, keep watering them well, and for greater success place a little bone meal in their holes.

The end of this month is not too late to plant or even sow runner beans and climbing French beans which are often got in far too early so then suffer the cold, the warmer soil now encourages much stronger better cropping plants.

Outdoors without cloches sow; peas, most Brassicas, lettuces and saladings, herbs, spinach, carrots, Swedes, salsify, scorzonera, kohl rabi, fennel, leeks, parsnips and hardy annual and biennial flowers.

Sow in situ outdoors but under cloches, plastic bottle cloches or even just jam jars; tomatoes, ridge cucumbers, gherkins, courgettes, marrows, pumpkins, French beans, runner beans and fast half hardy flowers.

Sow Trailing Nasturtiums in either the vegetable and / or flower garden for loads of colour, these are fairly problem free and every part is edible -especially the seeds which make fantastic pickles.

Any space left can be best filled with salads and annual herbs such as lettuce (especially loose leaf), endive, radish, dill, chervil and parsley.

If you have started off tomatoes, watermelons, pumpkins, squashes, ridge cucumbers and gherkins then these can be planted out now, preferably after hardening off and through black plastic or under cloches or cold-frames as these all love warmth.

The Brassica and leek plants already grown should be transplanted to their final sites in well enriched soil.

Harvest and use, or store and preserve any surplus crops before they go over.

Control asparagus beetle by leaving one plant uncut to form fern and attract all the eggs while cutting all others to the ground until the cutting season is over then promptly burning all the foliage of the sacrificial one.

Make night time inspections of your garden and especially the sowing and propagation area i.e. Go on a pest hunt with a torch for several nights running especially under the full moon.

LATE SPRING / MAY WILDLIFE & STOCK

Make more birdbaths as throughout summer birds eat much of our fruit and seedling leaves for their moisture not sustenance; a clean birdbath to wash and drink from saves much of their destruction. As young birds may now be fledging keep known-hunting-cats indoors as much of time as possible.
Inspect garden nets daily for trapped birds and hedgehogs.
Hens will almost certainly have hidden and hatched some chicks by now, ideally move mother and chicks to clean ground while these grow up.

LATE SPRING / MAY IN YOUR POTTING SHED

Don't forget to pot up, top dress, water and feed your house plants which tend to get forgotten in the rush this time of year.
Assess your house plants, then dispose of any that are not really satisfactory, better to care for the best well than dissipate your energy on too many.

LATE SPRING / MAY ORDER & BUY

Look for discounted leftover Early seed potatoes as there's still time for a good crop outdoors, or get these for putting aside (ideally in fridge) for summer or autumn planting for autumn and winter crops under cover.
Buy tender bedding plants now, there is still time for a good display and these will be happier in the warmer soil.

LATE SPRING / MAY IN YOUR GREENHOUSE

Have shading ready for greenhouse in case of heat waves, if so lucky.
Be extra vigilant with ventilation and prepare tender plants for hardening off by giving more ventilation for longer each day.
Search for parasitized aphids on rose leaves (look swollen and golden metallic) to move to greenhouse to control aphids there.
Examine each and every plant for pests and diseases; especially aphids, red spider mite and whitefly.
Pot up all greenhouse and container plants before it's too late.

Repot tomatoes deep to encourage basal roots.
Pot up more side-shoots removed from tomatoes to make free plants.
Feed indoor pot plants with liquid feed and or spray with diluted seaweed solution weekly.
The similar melon and cucumber plants need different treatment- melons need pollinating and often need their shoot tips nipping out to encourage fruiting while cucumbers are opposite, you need not nip out their tips nor pollinate, indeed remove all male flowers (no wee fruit behind it) or most indoor cucumbers will be bitter.
Plant out under walk-in cover; tomatoes, peppers, aubergines, melons, sweet corn, ridge cucumbers, courgettes and marrows.
Harden off tender plants for planting outside the second half of the month, stand these outdoors each day, bring in each night for three days or preferably more.
Statistically by the middle of the month we are past the danger of hard frost over most of the country so we can start putting out expensive tender plants such as citrus for the summer, initially clump these together and give them covers on cold nights.

Early Summer

At last it's June, a month of long light evenings, hopefully warm ones, but this month can also be cool and damp, it is dear old Blighty after all. Watering remains of course crucial and although the grass and weeds still need controlling the work load alters this month with a switch from sowing and planting to tending and in the flower garden cutting and dead-heading. The vegetable plot should be full with the greenhouse near emptied of the annual cropping plants now moved from pots into their final sites and the first harvests are coming in.

OUTDOORS IN YOUR GARDEN

Insure frequency of watering for all pot plants is at least daily preferably more often when hot and dry weather sets in!
Add seaweed solution and/or liquid feed directly into your water butt so your plants won't run short of food or any trace element as you water.
Rake mulches aside before rain comes so water reaches the soil then replace again immediately after.
Examine each and every plant for pests and diseases especially aphids and caterpillars, look under pots for slugs.
Ensure good weed control, make sure no weeds are getting away, hoe fortnightly if not weekly, don't forget to keep sharpening hoes.
Cut the grass at least fortnightly, preferably weekly, and raise the height of cut of the mower to a maximum as a longer grass stays greener a little longer through droughts.
Spray everything growing with diluted seaweed solution, and anything showing deficiency symptoms more heavily.
Deadhead bedding plants and cut back most flowering plants as their blooms fade.
Promptly dead head roses, prune these back to where the stalks divide then feed and water for an extra flush of blooms later.
Collect seed of spring flowers now set and fading, tie a paper bag over the heads so you don't lose the seed.

Tie in new growths of climbing plants and the same for tall herbaceous ones.

Fill up holes in your sunny ornamental beds with a tropical bedding display, still in their pots but submerged, of your tougher tropical house plants such as spider plants, Tradescantia, Monsteras and Colocasias, all of which can do really well outdoors.

Sow in any spare spot a mix of Night scented and Virginian stocks for colour and scent on warm late summer evenings.

Sow biennial and perennial flowers in a nursery bed or individual pots.

Barbecue season underway- save all bones, bake them on the ashes, pound to bits and add valuable phosphates to your compost.

Turn pond blanket weed into hanging basket liners and mulch mats.

Prevent moles pushing out new plants with huge 'pins' made from wire coat hangars or old bicycle wheel spokes (moles come as you water plants drawn by softer soil).

Soon the days will start drawing in- enjoy these long evenings while we have them so go out late on a warm night just to smell the evening scents.

EARLY SUMMER / JUNE IN YOUR FRUIT CAGE & ORCHARD

Spray well diluted seaweed solution on everything, but not during parching hot sun, better early morning or late evening.

Pick up and bury or burn all little fruits falling from trees, especially the pears, as these are often infested with grubs.

Stop the strawberry fruits being infected or contaminated with dirt by putting straw or shredded newspaper underneath, -or a jam jar pushed over fruit will keep the weather, slugs and birds off!

About the end of this month apples have June drop when surplus fruitlets are dropped to promote the rest, shake the trees to remove as many small fruits as possible, pick up and dispose of these chats.

Thin apricots and peaches, again, really ruthlessly so the remainder get bigger- never let two be near enough to touch as they swell.

Fruit thinning for other tree fruits and prize gooseberries- the first de-selection; remove every diseased, decayed, damaged, misshapen, distorted and congested fruitlet, compost or burn these rejects immediately, then protect remainder from birds and wasps.

Thin new raspberry canes to a hand's breadth apart, on average.

Blackcurrants can be pruned at the same time as picking- cut cropping branches back hard with the ripe fruit on them, you can then pick these elsewhere in more comfort.

Don't pick all your gooseberries, or red and white currants, all at once (and under ripe) protect some with umbrellas and net bags to fully ripen and become scrumptious.

Stone fruits, Prunus species, are traditionally pruned from now and before the end of next month to avoid Silver leaf; this includes cherries, apricots, peaches and plums, both flowering and fruiting ones.

Start Summer Pruning- that is; shorten most of the young growths by three quarters on most trained fruit trees and bushes to let in more light and air.

Prune grapevines back to three or five leaves after each flower truss and keep tying in the shoots for support.

EARLY SUMMER / JUNE IN YOUR VEGETABLE PLOT

Water everything generously, especially salad crops, sweet corn, beans, peas, potatoes and tomatoes, and even more-so when they are flowering.

Mark or dig up garlic before the leaves fade wither and disappear or you won't find all of it

Last chance to plant early seed potatoes for a decent crop, and a good time to be sowing more peas, runner and French beans.

It's not too late for a salad crop of turnips- if they don't do for you try adding bone meal when you sow.

Sow more successional crops (more small batches) of lettuces, radishes, spring onions and other saladings such as rocket, chervil, dill and beetroot, kohl rabi, Swedes, spinach, chicory, endive.

The end of this month the days grow longer again and then you can hope for more success sowing Pak choi and other Chinese greens and Florence fennel, but only if your soil is also really moist and rich.

Move any remaining transplant vegetables into the ground as soon as possible, especially leeks, Brassicas, squashes, tomatoes etc.

Green up any spare soil in the beds and borders as soon as possible- better a crop, flower or green manure than bare soil baking dry.

Remove any bolting (going to flower) beet or onions to prevent these 'encouraging' others.

Stop (nip out tip) of runner beans at top of support to make them bushier.

Although not strictly necessary it really helps sweet corn and peas if you draw the soil up around the haulm (stems) as this supports them and encourages bigger yields.

Give potatoes a really good soaking when you see their flowers appear as this is when the young tubers are swelling.

Go round nipping off the flowers from potato plants as this can increase yields, allegedly by a ton per acre.

Be sure to earth up main crop potatoes to keep light from reaching their swelling tubers- you can use soil, or layers of wet newspapers held down with whatever, or just grass clippings.

Fill aerosol caps or plastic cups with beer dregs, milk or fruit juice, bury to the lip and put them near the potato crop so the slugs can drown themselves.

Don't worry if an early variety of potatoes soon withers away- it's probably not blight, just normal as these are a quick crop and then need digging up.

Harvest and use, or store and preserve everything before it disappears

Courgettes (zucchini) should start to crop heavily from now on- inspect them every day and take each fruit when it is a tad on the small size and then you get many more- NEVER leave any to get big as this stops more forming.

Pick peas, beans, gherkins and sweet peas as fast as they come.

If you're finishing off a compost heap, add a thick layer of soil and a cold frame or cloche then plant a melon, squash or pumpkin in it for a wonderful crop.

EARLY SUMMER / JUNE WILDLIFE & STOCK

Do not forget to keep those birdbaths full or lose fruit in consequence of thirsty birds.

If you fit netting instead of bird scarers you will lose less fruit, however check netting daily for trapped birds and if it reaches the ground inspect for trapped hedgehogs.

Although I hate killing things if wasps are about in any number then put jammy jars half full of water with a foil lid pierced with pencil sized holes near ripening fruits, and also near windows to keep them away from kitchen.

Moles may appear wherever you water dry soil, either water everywhere or protect valuable plants with giant pins made from wire coat hangers or bicycle spokes pushed into the soil.

EARLY SUMMER / JUNE IN YOUR POTTING SHED

Don't forget to feed and water house plants which get neglected in summer.

Preserve, process and store as much produce as possible as now crops are coming in (which will all too soon cease) and you need to make your harvest last till next year.

EARLY SUMMER / JUNE ORDER & BUY

For Father's day, why not ask him if there's a job in the garden he's been avoiding and do it for him - if it's out of season give him an IOU until the right time.

Getting late but you can still buy ready grown small plants of all sorts of vegetables which just have time to crop before summer is over.

Not got enough soft fruit or want more trees, or roses etc. plan and order now for bare rooted plants for autumn planting.

EARLY SUMMER / JUNE IN YOUR GREENHOUSE

Examine each and every plant for pests and diseases especially aphids, red spider mite and whitefly.

Pot up everything left needing re-potting, add new canes and ties to support those in need.

Increase frequency of watering for most pot grown plants to at least thrice daily when the heat is on!

Feed indoor pot plants with comfrey or borage liquid or seaweed solution weekly.

Melons; must be pollinated, and thin fruits to get few but big ones.

Cucumbers; must NOT be pollinated, remove each and every male flower (no wee fruit behind them), and do not stop their shoots.
Pick ripe tomatoes promptly as if left to hang these reduce the size and number of others forming.
With large / beefsteak tomatoes reduce number to very few per plant or they will mostly be rather small.
You can place banana skins near ripening tomatoes to hurry them up.
Plant some early varieties of potatoes in big pots to grow under cover and then store in their pots to be 'new' potatoes for autumn and winter use.

Mid Summer

July, whimsically High Summer, the Dog days, a mythical time of heat which this month aspires to, however this is as often a cool wet month (please remember we are on a small island stuck between cold seas on the edge of a huge cold ocean). This, not later in autumn, is much more the gardener's month for harvesting most crops.

OUTDOORS IN YOUR GARDEN

Cut the grass at least fortnightly, preferably weekly, but raise the height of cut of mower to maximum as longer grass blades promote deeper roots keeping your lawn greener longer.
Lever out thistles, plantains and docks right now with a daisy grubber.
Make sure no weeds get away, but if weather stays dry you can probably get away with a hoeing fortnightly.
Water all pot grown plants at least thrice daily if it is hot!
For dried out baskets and planters and near thirsty plants in ground place a plastic bottle full of water with a tiny hole in it's bottom which will give very slow but effective watering that will soak in.
Or put ice cubes in plastic cup with a small drainage hole which will drip water to thirsty roots (but not for tender plants).
Rake mulches aside before rain showers to allow water to reach roots and replace them again after.
Feed plants in pots with comfrey liquid or seaweed solution weekly.
Spray everything growing with diluted seaweed solution, and anything with deficiency symptoms more heavily.
Give roses a feed and water after deadheading hoping for another flush if season proves long.
Deadhead all flowers as they go over unless wanted for seed (and do not save too many altogether or very many per plant).

When water butts get empty clean out and fit new sock (filter) to down pipe then they're ready to catch next rain, put that lovely black ooze on your compost.

After a barbeque put bones on the dying charcoal and bake them brittle then pound to dust before adding with ash to compost heap for valuable phosphates as well as potash.

Lift and divide spring bulbs now while they are dormant.

Turn pond blanket weed into hanging basket liners and mulch mats.

Tie in new growths of climbing plants.

Cut back evergreen and conifer hedges if sure there are no birds still nesting.

Sow 'biennials' before it's too late: foxgloves, stocks, hollyhocks and so on.

If you want the seeds for winter use cover ripening sunflower heads with bird-proof nets or paper bags or lose them.

MID SUMMER / JULY IN YOUR FRUIT CAGE & ORCHARD

Put paper bags over choice ripening fruits to keep wasps, birds and flies off.

Hang bottles of jammy water on fruit trees before their fruit ripens to catch wasp scouts which otherwise will go home and bring all their sisters.

Leave, indeed chop up, healthy windfall fruits to fob off wasps and birds.

Thin later cropping apples and pears again first removing the infected, infested, damaged, congested and odd, be ruthless.

Don't pick all soft fruit such as gooseberries under ripe, protect with nets and even cover with plastic umbrella to let some ripen fully.

Spread straw, bags of crumpled newspaper, old duvets, nets or sheets under valued fruit trees so dropping fruits don't bruise.

Prop heavily laden branches now, especially on plums, before they break.

Chop very heavy plum crops in half before they break branches.

Stone fruits, Prunus species, are traditionally pruned before the end of this month to avoid Silver leaf; this includes cherries, apricots, peaches and plums, both flowering and fruiting ones.

Summer pruning, remove half to three quarters of each new shoot, except for leaders, of red & white currants, gooseberries and all trained fruit.

Stop (nip out tip) the shoots of grapevines several leaves after bunches and remove or severely shorten all other surplus and non-fruiting shoots.

Then thin grapevine bunches to max of one per square foot or so of foliage, the more foliage to fruit the sooner, sweeter and better.

Blackcurrants need all old wood removing once fruited, raspberries likewise.

Start a new strawberry bed right now and it will establish well enough to crop well for you next year.

MID SUMMER / JULY IN YOUR VEGETABLE PLOT

Water crops in the vegetable bed heavily and often.

With courgettes and squashes never wet their flowers as causes rot.

Leeks need to put on a lot of bulk in the next months so make a trough alongside them and re-direct your grey water (recycled bath, shower and washing up water) to them twice a week.

As space becomes available when crops are harvested sow successional crops of chervil, rocket, hardy lettuce, lamb's lettuce, miner's lettuce, spring onions, winter radishes, turnips, beet, chards and spinaches, Pak-choi, Chinese cabbage and Florence fennel.

Sow suitable varieties of cabbages, kales and cauliflowers giving them plenty of space and water to get good plants to over-winter which will crop early next spring.

Dig potatoes as haulms die back, if blight appears cut off the haulms and wait a fortnight before digging them up.

Bury some new potatoes, deep, in shade or a cool damp place, in tin of sand, for winter treat.

Lay wet newspapers around main-crop potato haulms as mulch and to stop light greening protruding tubers.

Remove any flowers and seed pods on potato plants as these waste energy and removing them improves crops by a ton per acre.

Don't let courgettes, beans or sweet peas get away- keep picking them regularly and they'll keep producing, stop and so do they.

Earth up around base of sweet corn and tomato plants to add stability and encourage basal roots.

Hand pollinate sweet corn by running hands over (top) male tassels then over (lower) female silks- ideally of same variety only.

When harvesting cabbages leave a stump and cut a cross in it, then water and liquid feed well, side buds sprout and give bonus mini cabbage heads.

Cut sweet peas back hard and feed heavily for new 'tops' and more flowers.

Take almost all the pumpkin fruits off each plant leaving just the best to grow huge, likewise do not leave many squashes per plant.

Dig up garlic before all trace of their position departs with their dried leaves.

Do not bend down the leaves of ripening onions as this is counter-productive and causes rots later during storage.

However harvest onion crops as soon as their leaves wither

Lift your onions with a fork from underneath to break their roots if the tops have not died down naturally.

Harvest and use, store or process everything as soon as it's ready!!!!

Make a night time inspection of your garden especially round plants sustaining damage.

MID SUMMER / JULY WILDLIFE & STOCK

Thin ant colonies by putting tin cans over site and evicting 'eggs' in mid afternoon- hens, fish and birds love these.

Start saving seed heads especially such as grasses and of course sunflowers, to put out for the birds in winter.

When you're sure all fledglings have gone clean out bird boxes and compost old nests to destroy fleas and other parasites.

Now as they turn more to our fruit and eat less pests you can kill wasp nests without so many qualms.

Get point of lay pullets now so they will settle down and give eggs until well into winter.

MID SUMMER / IN YOUR POTTING SHED

Spread lavender and herb trimmings to sweeten your potting shed floor.
Clean out, air and ready your apple and root stores.
Process and preserve as much as possible, if over-whelmed freeze such as soft fruit to jam/jelly/ sorbet later when you have more time.

MID SUMMER / JULY ORDER & BUY

Buy your Japanese onion seed now so you have it ready for it's sowing window in late August as then it may be all sold out.
Order choice fruit trees and bushes, new varieties of ornamentals and other plants for autumn planting, leave it till later and the best may be gone.

MID SUMMER / JULY IN YOUR GREENHOUSE

Water, water, water.
Feed more lightly and change to more potash less nitrogen.
Leave ventilation fully open most of time.
Shade cucumbers if very bright and hot.
Pick tomatoes, aubergines and peppers as soon as ripe to prevent these suppressing more from forming.
Start new more productive plants of greenhouse cucumbers and melons by layering their tips in small pots.

Late Summer

August, this is often the kindest month for gardeners, warm and sunny, growth is slowing now, the pressures off, mostly harvesting to get on with, and oh yes- beware thunderstorms.

OUTDOORS IN YOUR GARDEN

Continue watering pot grown plants up to thrice daily especially if scorchingly hot.
Feed patio plants with diluted comfrey liquid or seaweed solution weekly.
Last month in which you should feed almost everything perennial as from end of month feeding will make any more growth too soft to over-winter.
Spray everything growing with diluted seaweed solution, and anything with deficiency symptoms more heavily.
Few weeds germinate now- but hoe, hoe, hoe fortnightly anyway.
Cut the grass at least fortnightly, preferably weekly and reduce the height of cut of the mower a little as you don't want weeds and tussock forming grasses getting away.
Deadhead roses and cut back most flowering plants as flowers fade.
Tie in new growths of climbing plants.
Trim back young shoots on Wistaria by roughly three quarters.
Cut leylandii and similar hedges now so re-growth is tough enough to stand through winter.
Plant out hardy biennial flowers for next year's blooms.
If off on a holiday exchange produce with friend for the watering.
Use driest period to repair, clean and paint metal gutters, pipes and tanks, roofs and do other repairs now before weather worsens.
Turn and re-mix your compost heap as it'll really cook this time of year.
Save seed heads of favourites for your own use, or packet them for presents.
Bored kids- get them grubbing weeds from lawn for proportionate treats.

LATE SUMMER / AUGUST IN YOUR FRUIT CAGE & ORCHARD

Leave grass to grow long under fruit trees for better fruits as it takes up water and nitrogen making fruit colour better and store longer.
If you didn't prune your blackcurrants when picking cut out at least third or more of oldest branches then water and feed generously.
Summer prune soft fruit and apples and pears further, remove three quarters of almost every young shoot except leaders (wanted for extensions).
Remove all runners from strawberries except those to pot up for new plants.
Early apples will be ripening- pick and use these before they go over, make apple puree and freeze, or juice, or dry.
Go over all your late apples and pears thinning out any misfits so the rest will be the better.
Don't leave ripe fruits to go to waste, pick and preserve them a.s.a.p.
Do not collect up all windfall fruits- chop some in half to leave to fob off the wasps and birds.
Put paper bags over prize peaches, pears and apples to keep flies, birds and wasps off.
Pick blackberries as soon as possible as they're then more digestible.
Plant out newly rooted strawberry runners and keep well watered.
Now is time to destroy wasp nests before they eat all your apples and pears- hire a professional!
Admit you have still left too many bunches on your grapevine and remove at least a third now to give the other's a chance...

LATE SUMMER / AUGUST IN YOUR VEGETABLE PLOT

Sow green manures and winter ground cover on any bare soil that is not mulched and once cleared of crops.
Sow Pak-choi, Miners, Lamb's, and loose leaf lettuces, saladings, spring onions, winter spinach, turnips, Chinese greens and hardy and biennial flowers (in situ for most of these).
Sow suitable and Japanese varieties of onions only in the last fortnight of this month for a much earlier crop next summer.
Nip tops off tomato plants as future flower trusses unlikely to ripen.
Gently lift pumpkins, melons and squashes onto pieces of wood or tile so they ripen off the damp soil.

Put stockings or tights or bags over ripening heads of sunflowers you want to save seed from so it's not eaten by birds.

If sweet corn cobs are stolen by badgers, rats or foxes once the silky threads dry and the cobs swell slip a topless bottomless tall beer can over each one then rub outside with smelly soap.

If your sweet corn goes over (the grains become firm to touch not creamy) the cobs can be left to dry to be stored and used in winter.

Keep picking courgettes, cucumbers, French and runner beans and sweet peas or they'll stop cropping, water well, and you can get another month or more of cropping.

Don't make it easy for slugs- dig all potatoes as soon as their tops wither.

Sort your potatoes as you dig them, store the best, save some nice tubers for next year's sets from healthy plants, and eat damaged and odd ones up first.

Start to get in early main crop potatoes as their haulms wither, late main crops can keep growing on into September for bigger yields.

Watch main crop spuds for any unearthing themselves and cover with soil or mulch to prevent greening.

If blight is a problem don't dig your spuds yet, cut the haulms off and dig up in a fortnights time once the spores have died off.

Ensure your onions are dried off really well, and garlic and shallots, use hot sunny days to dry off your onions- ideally in nets or even strung from the washing line, they'll then keep much better.

Pick and dry or freeze summer's herbs before they finish.

Harvest and use, store or preserve everything.

LATE SUMMER / AUGUST WILDLIFE & STOCK

Don't forget to put out water for the birds especially in dry spells.

Cut off and save ripening seed heads from almost any plant for feeding birds in winter especially oily ones such as sunflowers.

There's never a good time to clean a pond or pool, it always hurts wildlife but now is no worse than another, and at least it is pleasanter for you.

Cut sticks, especially hollow stemmed ones, into lengths, bind in bundles and hide these inside evergreens and hedges as nests for ladybirds and lacewings for winter.

LATE SUMMER / AUGUST UNDER COVER

Prepare and clean your apple, potato and root stores for filling next month.
Steep ripe plums or damsons in white rum, then add sugar syrup – it's better than sloe gin by a mile.
Dry apple rings, pear slices and sweet and hot peppers too.
Too many tomatoes to eat turn into puree/passata, bottle or freeze.
Make sure onions and garlic are storing nicely, remove rotters, those with thick necks are better used first or made into chutneys etc.

LATE SUMMER / AUGUST ORDER & BUY

Get those catalogues and order your soft fruit bushes and new fruit trees and ornamentals for planting in ONLY two months time.

LATE SUMMER / AUGUST IN YOUR GREENHOUSE

Root tips / cuttings of Pelargoniums into small pots to over-winter.
Plant up in big tubs or bags specially treated (or just some saved from the spring planting) seed potato sets and grow under cover for 'new' potatoes in winter.
Watch out for slug damage on and worse, in, ripening sweet and surprisingly hot peppers too.
Keep picking and processing greenhouse crops, they'll soon cease.
Start to get space ready to bring in tender plants in case weather turns cold early next month.

Early Autumn

September can have glorious weather, but it may also be wintery with gales, floods and early frosts. The last crops need gathering and it's sadly time to start preparing for winter. Use every daylight hour you can, do not forget how the light evenings soon disappear, and fast.

OUTDOORS IN YOUR GARDEN

- Decrease watering for pot and container plants, though still check them daily and also ensure drainage holes still free.
- Stop feeding, from now on it's more harm than good.
- Ensure no weeds are getting away, so hoe fortnightly and add extra mulch on top of any that's looking thin.
- Cut the grass at least fortnightly, preferably weekly, collecting the clippings with any fallen leaves and putting these around trees and bushes, raise the height of cut again by just a little each time.
- Transplant to their final positions biennial flowering plants both pot grown and those from a nursery bed with a decent rootball.
- Plant daffodils and most other spring flowering bulbs though not tulips yet.
- Sow hardy annuals to over winter and give earlier blooms.
- Sow bald patches in turf with grass seed, ideally prick over with a fork first then sow and brush the seed in, and add clover seed too.
- Sow green manures on any bare soil before the weather gets too cold for these to germinate well. And use easy to clear green manures: Limnanthes douglassi, Claytonia (Miners Lettuce) and Valerianella (Lamb's Lettuce).
- Don't stop deadheading autumn flowering plants as with luck there could yet be up to a dozen or more weeks of blooms to go.
- On still cold nights protect tender bedding plant displays from frost damage with sheets or newspaper and get more weeks of bloom.
- Cut back herbaceous plants only once their stems wither, and not to the ground but leave stubs to protect crowns.
- Make or add to the compost heap all the fading foliage and weeds before these wither, once less succulent they lose some value.

Check your tree stakes, ties and other supports as autumn often brings high winds.

This is probably the 'least bad' time to clean out a pool or pond as there is never a good time.

Suspend a net over your pool or pond to catch blowing leaves and stop them fouling the water and you'll need clean it less often.

Start an 'autumn leaves for mould' bin and keep adding to it, it's the best soil and compost improver you can get.

Bring tender plants in pots indoors as soon as any frost warning.

Citrus can stay out a bit longer than most tender plants if covered on frosty nights, and keep their roots from too much soaking by turning the containers on their sides during wet weather.

EARLY AUTUMN / SEPTEMBER IN YOUR FRUIT CAGE & ORCHARD

Let the grass grow longer under late apples for storing as it helps these keep better (takes up water and nitrogen) and cushions them if they fall.

Stretch blankets, duvets, sheets or nets or straw under favourite fruit trees to stop the windfalls bruising.

Pick plums as these ripen and drop, the wasps and birds will attack the ripest soonest so watch the little devils.

Pick pears differently to most fruit, do not let ripen on tree but pick a tad under-ripe, store in slightly moist warmth and eat as soon as ripe which is usually as colour yellows.

Pick the later ripening and storing apples only once they ripen- watch for ones starting to fall and then pick that whole tree.

Pick apples and pears wanted for keeping with their pedicel (little stalk) intact.

Don't let surplus apples or pears go to waste- dry, juice and puree them.

Put out squirrel scarers on nut trees (same as for birds but moved more often).

Rake under nut trees to find the nuts they've already buried.

Make blackberry jam before 'the devil spits on them' –before the spiny hooked seeds harden and become less digestible.

Knock down then burn, compost or deeply bury rotted and mummified fruits to protect next year's crop.

Put sticky bands around tree trunks to stop crawling pests going up and down during winter.

Wrap coarse cloth or crumpled corrugated cardboard in bands around fruit tree branches to trap pests looking for snug homes under rough bark, evict these later in winter.

Take cuttings of blackcurrants, redcurrants and gooseberries as their leaves fade and fall.

Remove old fruited canes of the raspberries, blackberries and hybrids as these go over and tie in the new ones.

Prune blackcurrants if not done already, and be ruthless with them.

Mow up leaves mixed with grass clippings and spread this under soft and tree fruit and shrubs as a mulch.

Plant some new fruit trees, bushes and shrubs over the coming weeks.

Re-check stakes, supports and ties before the weather turns stormy.

EARLY AUTUMN / SEPTEMBER IN YOUR VEGETABLE PLOT

Have sheets or newspapers ready to cover pumpkin and squash plants on coldest nights.

Cut pumpkins, marrows and squashes to store with a long, not short, piece of stem, then store on straw or in nets in a warm and dry place.

Pull up outdoor tomato and pepper plants to hang upside down in a dry place by their roots to ripen the last of the crop on them.

Dig up your remaining spuds on a drying sunny day as any increase in yield from now on will be cancelled by increasing pest damage.

Pick, shuck and dry sweet corn cobs that have gone over to give birds in winter, guard from damp and rats.

Plant out any available Brassicas, it's late but these may still bulk up.

Plant garlic and autumn shallots before the soil cools anymore.

Watch for volunteer garlic plants on their previous site, dig these up and replant them for next year's crop.

On bare soil sow spare and surplus pea, bean, sweet pea and lupin seed; all are legumes and leave free nitrogen when you hoe off their tops later in winter or spring.

Sow any other green manure on every bit of bare soil left.

Harvest and use, process or store everything quickly before it goes over.

EARLY AUTUMN / SEPTEMBER WILDLIFE & STOCK

Tie up bundles of woody and even thorny prunings and dried stems inside evergreens and hedges to make insect hotels.
(To make these bundles- lay pair roughly yard/metre long pieces of wire or similar, parallel and foot/ half metre or so apart, cut prunings to roughly yard/metre lengths and lay across these wires, once a pile wind wires tightly around to pull bundle together and knot well, optionally add extra layers of cardboard or paper for insulation and plastic outer wrap against excess wet.)
Carefully empty then clean pest and disease ridden material out of existing bird boxes (be careful stuff can carry nasties, still okay for compost).
Round out the corners of rectilinear nest boxes with plaster so nests can't deform (eggs may then fail to turn and 'stick').
When cutting back stems with seed heads on them bash these against a post or similar to liberate the seed for the birds and other critters.
Make toad holes of large pots or similar set on side well into side of pond and pool banks making deep damp caves, conceal with turves.

EARLY AUTUMN / SEPTEMBER IN YOUR POTTING SHED

After cleaning tools that you are putting away for winter wipe down with an oily rag (and as I use my old frying oil I can find my tools in the dark by the smell of chips).
Watch out for rodent invasion into sheds, greenhouses, and attics as nights cool, take suitable precautions.
Especially put mouse traps where you store your seeds particularly nuts, sunflower seeds, dried sweet corn, peas and beans.
Go through your seeds reserving those few that may yet be sown but putting all the rest -if worth keeping- in cool, dry rodent proof place (I find a dead refrigerator superb for this).
Put slug pubs (plastic cups of beer/fruit juice/milk) in potato and root stores- you may be surprised how many you catch! Put mouse traps there as well, just in case.
Marrows, quashes and pumpkins often rot where they rest; hang in a net or make a 'mattress' for them of straw or shredded paper.

Sort stored onions and other stored alliums into good and 'use now', large quantities going over should be processed, pickled, made into chutneys, curry and sauce bases or fried in oil and frozen.

On dry sunny days move stored garlic, shallots and onions outdoors to air so they will keep longer. I find large onions keep less well than small and rather oddly either keep longer stored upside.

Prepare your long term apple storage ready; plenty of shredded newspaper, boxes or trays, and ideally a dead fridge or freezer to put them in. Put a mouse trap there, again just in case. (If you foolishly store windfall apples put slug traps in with them as well!)

EARLY AUTUMN / SEPTEMBER ORDER & BUY

If you haven't yet got the catalogues and ordered more bare rooted fruit trees and bushes do so now for October planting.

Look for hardy chrysanthemums going over and now sold off cheap - get these, cut them back hard, keep in a cool greenhouse or cold frame, pot on in spring for a fantastic show next autumn.

Watch out for remaindered sacks of bar-b q charcoal, it will burn just as well next summer.

EARLY AUTUMN / SEPTEMBER IN YOUR GREENHOUSE

Stop regularly watering most tender plants under cover, from now on give them just enough to stop wilting.

Sow chervil, rocket, hardy and loose-leaf lettuce, lamb's lettuce, miner's lettuce, Pak-choi, spring onions, winter radishes and carrots in pots and trays.

It's worth the gamble to sow carrots, mangetout peas and even French beans, it all depends on weather, light and warmth.

Take the growing tips and flowers off greenhouse tomato plants as no more growth or fruit will be any use.

Clean all the glass of coldframes and greenhouses that will have plants in them during the darker days ahead.

Move out grapevines and other plants under cover for ripening once they go over.

Bring under cover tender plants and herbs you want to save if you've not already.

Pot up mint plants, with as much rootball as possible for forcing under cover.

Mid Autumn

October, some warm but wan days, gales and often floods, frosts likely. The days are short so use every good hour to get the pruning, tidying and winter preparations done in case the weather closes in sooner than expected.

OUTDOORS IN YOUR GARDEN

Make sure no weeds are getting away, so still hoe fortnightly preferably when the wind is drying.
Continue to cut the grass at least fortnightly, preferably weekly, return some clippings and shredded leaves to turf to feed the worms for better fertility, drainage and aeration.
Brush leaves onto the lawn, shred and collect these with the lawn clippings using a rotary mower, make these into rings around trees and bushes or pack into dustbin bags, put somewhere dark and in a year or two they're excellent mulch.
Raise the height of cut on your mower a little more each cut to leave the grass blades much longer as these will then endure winter better and be a fund of material to cut in spring.
Sow grass seed over any bare patches before soil cools.
Aerate and spike your grass as needed (where it's become compacted) brushing in sharp sand and grass seed afterwards, for best results scarify whole area thoroughly beforehand.
Cut and move turves to repair edges and bald patches, to make new beds and borders or grass over old ones.
If you are saving urine to add to your compost or as a fertilizer add some sugar and it will stay sweeter and not whiff so much.
Last chance to sow hardy annual seed for an early show next year, sow on soil then cover with layer of old potting compost as this reduces weeds.
Lots of bonfires and fireworks coming, if it's dry weather liberally hose down anything that might catch fire from a spark especially conifers, evergreens and bushy climbers.

Now is a good time to plant almost anything hardy: bulbs, deciduous shrubs, trees and herbaceous perennials so fill in or rework any gaps in your beds and borders.

When planting trees and bushes dig holes well before these arrive to let more air into the soil- and also they can be put in more speedily.

Admit an Indian summer is now unlikely (though original Indian summers would be next month), put away your garden furniture with a wipe down, wax or oil where appropriate.

Make your garden tidier putting everything unnecessary out of sight, if necessary create a 'glory hole' somewhere, or stack the 'stuff' up and hide it with a waterproof cover.

Move fallen leaves before they choke low growing plants and knock off accumulations on evergreens and conifers.

Make compost with all the dying back foliage, weeds and crop residues before these have withered away and lost value.

Place a warm insulated waterproof cover on top of your compost bin contents (e.g. plastic bag of newspaper balls).

Put away plastic hose, watering cans and anything that holds water before hard frosts come and freeze them as this both makes them brittle and expansion breaks them.

Insulate outdoor pots and containers of marginally hardy plants with bubble wrap or similar, do not impede drainage.

Empty and clean, and get more and fit, water butts and gutters now to catch winter rain for next spring and summer.

Go on a Coral Spot hunt as the leaves drop- look for pink spotted stems and cut these out and burn them.

Check straps, tree ties and stakes as the coming weeks may have the most powerful gales of year.

Cut back herbaceous plants as their stems wither but leave stumps to catch leaves and show position if it snows.

Put sharp sand over crowns of dying down herbaceous plants to exclude slugs and discourage weeds.

Put mats of dry leaves over slightly tender herbaceous plant crowns and hold these down with a layer of grass clippings.

Put dead sticks, fern or bracken around and amongst the crowns of tender plants left outdoors as this will help them survive cold better.

Spread mulches under and around everything possible.

MID AUTUMN / OCTOBER IN YOUR FRUIT CAGE & ORCHARD

The very latest apples may hang till now but need picking and storing before hard frosts or birds damage them.
Gather grapes needing picking before the weather worsens.
Get your soft fruit, shrubs and trees planted soon and before the soil loses all it's warmth.
Winter prune apples, pears, and most other trees as soon as they drop their leaves, but don't touch the stone fruits
Winter prune soft fruits thinning out blackcurrant bushes, removing dead raspberry and bramble canes and cutting back side shoots on gooseberries and currants.
Prune grapevines a.s.a.p. even if all their leaves haven't fallen yet.

MID AUTUMN / OCTOBER IN YOUR VEGETABLE PLOT

Plant garlic and autumn shallots sooner rather than later this month, while the soil still has some warmth.
You can damage the basal plate (where the roots emerge) planting shallots and garlic cloves by just pushing them into place so dib a wee hole first.
Plant garlic cloves a little under the surface, ideally surround each with a weather protection tube cut from a plastic bottle.
Shallots grow best projecting out of the soil, hold the sets in place whilst rooting with a wee mound of soil or potting compost to be removed later.
Sow hardy broad beans and peas for really early crops hoping for a mild winter, under cloches will give more likely success.
You can plant (they'll have to be your own saved ones) potato sets now, a tad deep then cover over and after that add a thick layer of straw or leaves and most years that's it to crop earlier next year.
Protect over-wintering Brassicas against the wood pigeons, empty inverted wire hanging baskets work well!
Cover up carrots with some shredded paper or straw then a plastic sheet so you can dig them when the ground is frozen.
If you grow celery you need to cover it over with straw and plastic in addition to the usual earthing up as this is not hardy.

On bare soil empty out opened and unwanted packets of flower seeds, if they grow they'll make a fine green manure, if they don't it will have saved you sowing them next spring.

MID AUTUMN / OCTOBER WILDLIFE & STOCK

Cut hollow stemmed prunings into foot length bundles, wrap each round with newspaper leaving ends open and tie inside evergreens or conifers for insect hotels.
Collect and dry seeds and berries not for sowing next year but to feed birds.
Clean and refill bird baths, and start using warm water.

MID AUTUMN / OCTOBER IN YOUR POTTING SHED

B.S.T. ends this month, longer darker nights, fit a good padlock to your garden shed to baffle 2-legged rats.
Check ripening pears daily, as yesterday they were under-ripe, tomorrow they'll have gone over!
Place your longest storing apples on straw or shredded paper rather than on a hard surface, and the same goes for squashes and ideally hang these in nets.
Store marrows and pumpkins in a warm dry place to ripen their skins, a shed is not as good as under the bed.
Go through your stores evicting anything rotting and threatening others.
Put slug pubs in where your potatoes are stored to draw out the blighters if you have not already.
Likewise top up slug pubs in where your apples are stored especially if you collect windfalls.
Carefully position mousetraps where your seeds and bulbs are stored but so kids and cats won't come amiss.
On cold wet days overhaul your tools, clean and oil the metal and sand down and oil or paint the wood, also paint on your post code obviously and again in another place less obviously.

MID AUTUMN / OCTOBER ORDER & BUY

A second hand ski suit makes cold days workable, tell local charity shops you want one.

Make and slip carpet offcut insoles into your wellies for heavenly comfort.

Not to late to order bare rooted fruit trees and soft fruit to plant soon, likewise shrubs and herbaceous plants.

Order seed catalogues to peruse at leisure.

Order seed potatoes a.s.a.p. as there's often a shortage of the new good varieties.

Order point of lay pullets to arrive next month and they'll give you eggs soon after mid-winter once they've settled down.

Stake a claim now on wood ashes about to be produced from nearby bonfires over Halloween and Fireworks night- ideally clean woody ones not from those burning 'nasties'.

Look for end of season 'sale' bar-b-q charcoal as it keeps fine till next year when it will undoubtedly cost more, some can be pounded to coarse powder to improve sowing and potting composts, darken soil, and small lumps make good drainage at the bottom of pots

Buy Poinsettias and 'Christmassy' plants now to enjoy them for a month and more before giving them away as presents…

MID AUTUMN / OCTOBER IN YOUR GREENHOUSE

Bring in any not hardy plants a.s.a.p. before cold weather hurts them.

Tender plants now under cover may roast on the odd hot days- check auto ventilation is working or open up in time.

Check your greenhouse heater does come on and go off as you imagine.

Decrease watering further to a minimum as growth slows more, keep humidity down to prevent moulds, never splash water about.

Be extra vigilant to remove every dead leaf and bloom as it is on these grey mould may start.

Go on an undercover pest hunt; turn them out of their cosy dens, a portable car vacuum cleaner will catch those fast moving wood lice.

Drain and insulate greenhouse and outside pipes, taps and hoses before harder frosts come.

Clean all glass and plastic again to let through the most of the dim autumn light.

Sow Claytonia (Miner's Lettuce) or Valerianella (Corn salad) as green manure in greenhouse and walk in tunnel borders.
Spread straw on paths under cover as this lets droplets through and prevents most re-evaporating.

Late Autumn

November, although there may be warm spells the days are now very short, use these wisely, get jobs done before worse weather comes.

OUTDOORS IN YOUR GARDEN

Water pot grown evergreens especially if stood in dry positions and also check drainage holes.
Make sure weeds never get away, so hoe when soil conditions allow. Add extra mulch on top of thinning ones.
Cut the grass as long as it keeps growing collecting the fallen leaves with the clippings or raking them onto now empty or dormant beds and borders.
Give your last cut then send mower for servicing ready for next year.
Lime tough grass swards (only if no Ericaceous plants nearby) with garden lime a.k.a. ground chalk to discourage acid loving weeds such as speedwell and buttercups.
Collect every scrap of available material and make compost before real cold weather arrives.
Turn cooked compost heaps, sieve and store mature compost.
This is a windy month so check fences, tree stakes and straps before and after gales.
Cover slightly tender subjects left in ground with bracken, fleece or even a mound of chunky bark but never wrap in plastic sheet.
Check and re-label trees and shrubs- wooden clothes pegs and pencil used firmly last longer than most alternatives.
Finish pruning trees, roses and shrubs before colder weather comes.
Plant out bare rooted deciduous shrubs, trees and roses if soil is in good condition.
Getting late but can still take cuttings of easy subjects, Buddleija, roses and so on so do so now!
Sow green manures or annual flowers on any bare soil, may be too late but try anyway.
Get any remaining daffodil and tulip bulbs planted as soon as possible.
Cover crowns of vulnerable plants with sharp sand versus late slugs.

Don't tidy back herbaceous flowering plants until the stems have withered or the plant loses nutrients.

Do tidy away withered back herbaceous tops but leave long stubs to protect new shoots.

Dig, split and replant herbaceous plants rather than rush in spring.

Put a sieved mulch of spent potting compost over patches of bulbs and crowns of died down herbaceous plants to prevent weeds germinating there.

Weed and tidy now before a hectic social season robs your time.

Grab those ashes from clean bonfires once they're cool and keep dry till needed for the garden- or simply spread around old trees.

Collect up garden canes and store somewhere really dry, say a roof-space, so they'll keep for another year not rot where they stand.

Have a bucket of sharp sand ready to sprinkle on icy and slippery paths and stepping stones to give secure footing.

Take all remaining hosepipes and plastic watering cans, empty pots etc. under cover before hard frosts make them too brittle to move.

Put a football or plastic bottle in ponds or pools to keep a hole as it bobs when ice forms.

Go on, clean the muck and dead leaves out of the pool!

Empty and clean out gutters and water butts, and fit or renew sock filter on down-pipe.

LATE AUTUMN / NOVEMBER IN YOUR FRUIT CAGE & ORCHARD

Get any unfinished pruning done, especially grapevines, and it's still time to root vine cuttings.

A bit late but you can still take and root cuttings of most soft fruit.

Cut young shoots from choice fruit trees to keep cool, damp and dark for grafting next spring.

With bare branches now check usually hidden ties are not getting too tight as wood will have swelled since last year!

Plant out bare rooted fruit trees and soft fruit if soil is in good condition.

If soil frozen or waterlogged put bare rooted plants in tubs or bags of moist potting compost (you recover the compost later when you plant out).

Touch up sticky tree bands on trunks of fruit trees versus crawling pests and likewise add more cardboard or cloth band traps.

LATE AUTUMN / NOVEMBER IN YOUR VEGETABLE PLOT

Lime the vegetable beds, ideally one quarter of vegetable plot each year, best before Brassicas or Legumes never just before potatoes
It's getting too late to plant garlic in open, better do so in pots under cover.
Twist the top off Brussel's sprout plants then the sprouts swell more.
Dig some carrots to keep in a cool and dark place in case of hard frosts freezing ground solid.
In colder areas or if very cold weather is predicted harvest and store under cover winter cabbages, leeks and most root vegetables though leave parsnips in as frost improves their flavour.

LATE AUTUMN / NOVEMBER WILDLIFE & STOCK

Fill bird baths with fresh water on frozen mornings so the birds can have a drink and keep this topped up and de-iced.
Put up some new bird boxes and clean out old ones (be careful –full of nasties!) ready for prospective lodgers in the coming year.
Start feeding birds with seeds and so on especially in coldest weather.
Lay old carpet or similar on ground and move every few days to reveal lots of treats which come up to surface for birds.
Make sure your hens are snug, warm and dry with plenty of straw.

LATE AUTUMN / NOVEMBER IN YOUR POTTING SHED

Go through stored fruit and vegetables- remove rotting ones and look for fresh pest damage- if any use slug pub or mouse trap as indicated.
Customise your potting shed- make it snugger, cosier and quieter- line the walls with old carpet, even the ceiling and put several layers on the floor.
Prepare aluminum cans now for anti-slug barriers in spring- neatly cut off top and bottom and divide into circular bands, work these even nastier with spikes when cut with pair of pinking shears.
As you get new seed packets for next year put them in a tin box in a cool dry dark place so they don't go off.

Go through your old seed packets and throw out those which failed this year or are opened and more than a few years old.
Put unused unopened out of date seed packets in well sealed plastic container and deeply bury as a time capsule for future interest.

LATE AUTUMN / NOVEMBER ORDER & BUY

Send in your seed orders NOW if not done so already.
Look for discounted Halloween goods such as fake spiders that will make great bird scarers next spring.
Stake your claim on the ashes of any bonfire you see and get them before they're wet.
Winter festivities only a month away so get pot grown holly, Skimmia and Mahonia plants to use as live decoration in cool rooms.
Buy nice houseplants for gifts now; and enjoy them a month for free!
Buy a Lonicera fragrantissima in a large pot –even if you never plant it this will give delicious flowers for months from deepest winter on.
Order fruit trees for mid December delivery for gifts for friends.

LATE AUTUMN / NOVEMBER IN YOUR GREENHOUSE

On warm days ventilate greenhouse, tunnel and coldframe plants as much as possible.
Only water when plants desperate for it, and never splash it about.
Keep your watering can full indoors near a radiator or other warm place so you give your plants less of a shock when you water them.
Sow spring onions, radishes and rocket in pots on sunny windowsills.
Inspect plants under cover carefully remove every dead leaf, stem, twig or flower as it is on these mould will most often start.
And again clean greenhouse glass inside and out as dirt reduces light significantly, then clean cloches and cold frame glass/plastic as well.

Early Winter

December is when winter starts to bite, the days are really short, the year's coming to an end, be guilt free and get all those jobs done now before the weather closes in, so never waste a single dry moment.

OUTDOORS IN YOUR GARDEN

Check fences, tree straps, ties and stakes after each gale.
If you have any spring bulbs still not planted then hurry up or as it's so late put them in pots undercover to plant out in spring.
Plant out hardy trees and bushes only when soil is in good (friable) condition never if waterlogged or frozen.
Prune back to half dozen or so buds Wistaria shoots already shortened in summer.
Do major pruning work to trees and bushes but not to ornamental stone fruits or evergreens and leave untouched hollow stemmed shrubs such as Buddleia till spring as water lodges in the holes.
Cut timber for firewood, preferably when moon is waning.
Cut any hedges not trimmed during summer.
Make a bonfire of diseased and thorny material, save charcoal for barbecues and ashes for applying in spring.
Cut the grass only if weather is very mild; collect last fallen leaves with any clippings and plastic bag these to turn into leaf mould. (Pee in bags of leaves and they rot much quicker.)
Lime most tough grass swards every other year but not near or amongst Ericaceous plants and other lime haters.
Put empty hanging baskets over particularly valued soon to be emerging bulbs or herbaceous plant crowns so they won't be accidentally stood on if snowed over.
Place an insulating cap of empty hanging baskets full of dry leaves or fern over the crowns of dormant tenderer plants such as Dahlias.
Try a Victorian trick to make empty borders seasonally attractive by pushing into the soil pieces of evergreen prunings, preferably those with cheerful foliage, flowers or berries.
Clean out gutters and drains now the last leaves have fallen.

Place or replace an old sock on each downpipe to catch debris washed down by rain.

Take remaining hosepipes and plastic watering cans, empty pots etc. under cover but not when hard frosts make them too brittle to move.

Have a bucket of sharp sand ready to sprinkle on icy and slippery paths and stepping stones to give secure footing.

Get your appetite back- turn your compost heap, all out onto a sheet, wet it then repack it all well mixed up, and what an apt end to a year.

EARLY WINTER / DECEMBER IN YOUR FRUIT CAGE & ORCHARD

On a bright day use a long cane to knock off mummified and rotten fruits to stop these over-wintering pests and diseases.

Re-touch or make sticky bands round fruit tree trunks to stop crawling pests such as Winter moth.

Wrap new cloth or cardboard bands around trunks to trap crawling pests and remove and compost any old ones.

Tie nets or black cotton over cherries, plums and gooseberries if bullfinches are common as these rip off their flower buds.

Do get any remaining pruning done a.s.a.p. especially of grapevines.

Take nets off fruitcages as heavy snow may break it or the supports.

EARLY WINTER / DECEMBER IN YOUR VEGETABLE PLOT

Dig some carrots and leeks (and some parsnips if already frosted), pack in slightly damp sand in a shed in case the ground becomes frozen solid and impossible to dig for months.

Or cover carrots, leeks and cabbages left in ground with thick layer of leaves or shredded paper and then a plastic sheet well held down- so you can still get at them when the ground elsewhere is frozen solid.

Dig parsnips and leave these on surface for frost to sweeten them before use.

Lay nets over Brassicas, especially in hard weather, to deter wood pigeons.

EARLY WINTER / DECEMBER WILDLIFE AND STOCK

Float a football or plastic bottle one quarter full in a pool or pond to bob and keep a hole open through ice to let noxious gases escape.
Don't forget to regularly wash and refill birdbaths and put food out for the birds and more often the harder the weather.
Regularly clean bird feeders to stop these spreading diseases.
Clean out bird boxes (to remove parasites) and put up some more.
Give your chickens any green fodder you can glean as they will be desperate for some.

EARLY WINTER / DECEMBER IN YOUR POTTING SHED

Go on tidy your shed and get rid of all the junk and defunct tools.
To help dispose of those unwanted unopened seed packets you just can't let go of; seal them in a glass or plastic container and bury them as a time capsule.
Process fading stored apples before they go over- apple puree is useful in all sorts of Christmassy dishes.
Use sweet potatoes and squashes up as these will not keep well for much longer.
Save tinsel and garish plastic wrappings for bird scarers next year.
After parties half empty bottles may not be worth drinking- but are worth putting aside for slug pubs come spring.
Stop seasonal opportunists; fit good locks to your sheds and garage.

EARLY WINTER / DECEMBER ORDER & BUY

Purchase sand, grit, salt, a stiff brush and shovel and then by sod's law we should be safe from another very hard icy winter.
Order potato and onion sets, onion and leek, celery and early tomato seeds as soon as possible as all these will be soonest needed.
Order evergreens, soft fruit and herbaceous plants for early spring planting.
Have no Citrus? These are valuable producing fresh fruits in winter, so treat yourself, most value I reckon are a Meyers lemon, and a tangerine/satsuma.
Want even more winter greenhouse fruits then the Strawberry or Cherry Guava, Psidium cattleianum crops well and is treated much as a citrus.

And the Physalis Cape Gooseberry is another good winter cropper if kept frost free.
Get some variegated evergreens such as holly, Elaegnus, Euonymous etc. in pots as seasonal decoration, especially good on windowsills.
Buy your friends and neighbours packets of seed (of your favourite flower or vegetable) or those with appropriate names.
Mistletoe (becomes cheaper from Christmas eve) buy some with good berries then stand in water in a cool airy bird proof place so the berries ripen well to stick on your trees in Spring.
Immediately after xmas all exotic fruits they did not sell will reduce in price- just think of each as a packet of interesting seeds within a free fruit- dates, avocados, pawpaws, custard apples, tamarinds, mangoes et al- all fun to try.

EARLY WINTER / DECEMBER IN YOUR GREENHOUSE

Put up extra insulation as coldest days to come though shortest darkest ones are over.
On a bright day carefully inspect greenhouse plants for mealy bugs, scales, aphids and moulds as these easily prosper unnoticed.
Only use warm water and only water if plants are desperate.
Know when to water Citrus- feel their fruits, if softening do water them, but be sure they're well drained, don't forget- rain water only.
Sow some mustard and cress seed a week before xmas on damp kitchen roll paper on plates to add fresh greens to those turkey sandwiches.
Risk a sowing under cloches or in greenhouse border or in pots in warmth of: rocket, loose leaf winter hardy lettuces, radish, turnips, Chinese mustard greens, spring onions and pak-choi.
Plant some extra early Early variety potato sets, each in a huge pot, and keep in a warm light place for a very early, if small, crop.
Relax, take it easy for a while; note your successes and mishaps of this year, plan to grow more or less accordingly, then enjoy the fruits of your labours, and hope for as much pleasure again next year.

Tables of expected production

Many vegetable books offer some idea of expected yields, remember these cannot be taken as more than guide lines as yields can vary totally. Some years all of a crop fails and another year you're eating it till it's coming out your ears. Still it is necessary to make a comparison of crops to help with initial planning. You must decide roughly how much ground to give to each crop. So I've made a table to rate the various vegetables according to their average returns for effort. But it is only a rough guide; in most soils, in an average year, with a careful gardener. Ideally the same row or block will produce the relative amounts shown in the table, more with more sun and water and little at all in a miserable season! Potatoes and runner beans and courgettes give you high yields for the space whereas peas and garlic give small yields by weight -but higher by value!

Thus any table is only a very rough guide to judge which crops are best to grow for saving work and time and an even rougher guide to judging the monetary value of a crop as one can never give truly comparable cash returns for any crop. The price of vegetables fluctuates with the earliest being most valuable and then prices fall as main-crops mature. Local scarcities and gluts change potential cash value many fold. Generally though such as courgettes, broccoli and French beans are very expensive to buy compared to the cost of growing them while most roots and main crop potatoes are incredibly cheap to purchase, even organic ones. Peas and sweet corn are time consuming to grow and process but the bought articles are never ever anywhere near as good as your own. Ultimately quality especially freshness is only obtainable from your own garden and the latter is particularly important for the lettuces and saladings which rapidly lose their crispness, and sweet corn, peas and new potatoes. Maybe onions, roots and main crop potatoes are better bought unless time and ground are amply available. Where space is at a premium then the best all round value comes from herbs, salad vegetables and climbing peas and beans. If time is very limited then squashes, beans and early potatoes can all be grown with little work or attention. Onion sets, garlic and shallots are equally easy and take little time providing your weed control is good. Likewise for the roots -if you sow them well in the first place.

As this is necessarily a very approximate guide when you find that there are just not enough or far too many peas, carrots or whatever produced from your first season then plan to devote more or less space the next year.

This table indicates whether each crop is hard, moderate or easy to grow well and cleanly <u>to the same quality as</u> supermarket produce. This varies enormously with soil and situation and it is unlikely your plot will grow both carrots and cauliflowers well as the former needs a light sandy soil and the latter a heavy rich clay. However I have assessed each crop according to whether or not it is usually easy or not to produce a harvest bearing in mind their needs and common pests and diseases.

I have further indicated whether each crop takes more or less actual time to be raised and prepared to the same state as you would find it for sale (though of course yours is a lot lot fresher!).

Then an indication of whether each crop costs you less or much less to grow than to be bought.

The biggest expense is the seed, some special hybridised seeds (Often F1) can be incredibly expensive so total costs vary much more if you save your own seed or buy the highly promoted 'own brand' seeds instead of standard varieties.

However not all crops are easy to save suitably pure seed from without isolation so this is indicated in the final column.

Yield- A fair crop to expect: Huge, Good, Moderate or Light growing in poor / heavy soils.
Ease- Will it be Hard, Moderate or Easy to grow well & clean as shop bought
Time- Is it Time consuming, Moderate or Quick to grow well & clean as shop bought
Saving- Will your own likely be a Mistake, a Good deal or hugely Cheaper compared to buying the shop equivalent
Own- Will it be even Better value when home saved seed or offsets are used, or does this require Care, or is it downright Difficult to do so effectively.

Crop	Yield poor / h	Ease	Time	Saving	Own
Beans, Broad	Mod./Good	Easy	Quick	Good	Better
Beans, French	Good/Good	Mod.	Mod.	Cheaper	Better
Beans, Runner	Huge/Huger	Easy	Time	Cheaper	Better
Beetroot	Mod./Huge	Mod.	Mod.	Cheaper	Difficult
Broccoli	Light/Good	Hard	Mod.	Cheaper	Difficult
Brussel's sprout	Light/Good	Hard	Time	Cheaper	Difficult
Cabbages	Mod./Good	Easy	Mod.	Cheaper	Difficult
Cauliflowers	Light/Good	Hard	Mod.	Cheaper	Difficult
Carrots	Good/Mod.	Hard	Time	Cheaper	Difficult
Celery	Light/Good	Hard	Time	Mistake	Care
Celeriac	Light/Good	Mod.	Mod.	Good	Care
Courgettes	Huge/Huge	Easy	Quick	Cheaper	Difficult
Cucumber, Ridge	Mod./Mod.	Mod.	Quick	Good	Difficult
Garlic or Shallot	Light/Mod.	Easy	Quick	Good	Better
Kohlrabi	Mod./Good	Easy	Mod.	Cheaper	Difficult
Leeks	Light/Huge	Hard	Mod.	Cheaper	Care
Lettuces	Light/Mod.	Mod.	Mod.	Cheaper	Care
Onions	Mod./Good	Mod.	Time	Good	Care
Parsnips	Mod./Mod.	Mod.	Mod.	Good	Care
Peas	Light/Mod.	Easy	Time	Good	Better
Potatoes	Good/Huge	Easy	Mod.	Good	Better
Radishes	Light/Light	Mod.	Quick	Cheaper	Care
Spinach's	Mod./Mod.	Mod.	Time	Cheaper	Care
Squashes	Mod./Mod.	Easy	Quick	Cheaper	Difficult
Sweet corn	Light/Good	Easy	Time	Good	Difficult
Swedes	Light/Mod.	Mod.	Quick	Good	Care
Tomatoes	Huge/Good	Mod.	Time	Cheaper	Care
Turnip	Mod./Good	Mod.	Mod.	Cheap	Difficult

Table of what to do to which crop when

This table is about the timing for sowing and planting crops, the year is divided into four seasons, then into each as early, mid and late, making 12 periods equivalent to the months with Winter covering December, January and February and so on. It is based on East Anglia, obviously in colder later regions or more exposed sites the timing will be later. Please adjust, it is only a guide to what I achieve without too much skill, a keen gardener can have almost any crop any time with enough effort.

Key to table-

Sow warm- means the time to start sowing in a heated propagator under cover in a frost free well lit space, ideally with extra light.

Sow u/c- is time to start sowing under unheated cover be it glass or plastic.

Sow o/s- is time to start sowing direct in situ or in a seedbed outdoors in the soil.

Plant u/c- is time to move modular grown plants into cropping containers or beds and borders under cover.

Plant plot- is time to put modular grown plants in open ground, after hardening off or with extra protection such as a cloche.

Harvest- is when you can expect picking a crop to commence. (Bear in mind there are Early, Mid and Main crop varieties of most vegetables which will alter the harvest period immensely, as will differences in moving and transplanting times which can check crops holding the harvest back. Also you can take most crops immature at the same time as making space for remainder to fill out.)

BSL a **B** means it's necessary to sow batches of new plants to get successive crops, a **S** means store the crop for winter use, and an **L** means that crop can be left in ground till required (most winters).

Sow		Sow	Plant	Plant	Harvest	Harvest	BSL
warm	u/c	o/s	u/c	o/s	u/c	o/s	
Bean, Broad	1	2-3	3-4	3	3	4	6	B
" hardy	-	11	11	2	-	4	5	B
Bean, French	3	4-5	5-7	4	5-8	5	7-9	BS
Bean, Runner 3	4	5-6	4		5-7	6	7-9	S
Bean, Soya	3	3	-	4	5-6	6-9	7-9	B
Beetroot	2	3	4-6	4	4-6	4	6-10	BS
Broccoli	2	3	4-6	-	5-7	-	8-10	B
"calabrese	2	3	3-4	-	4-5	-	7-11	B
" sprouting	-	3-4	-	4-5	-	2-4	BL	
Brussel's 2	3	3-4	-	5-7	-	10-12	BL	
Cabbages	2	3	3	3	4	6-8	7-11	BSL
" spring	-	6-8	7	-	7-8	-	3-5	BL
" Savoy	-	3	4	-	4-5	-	12-3	BL
Cauliflowers 3	3	4	-	5	-	9-11	B	
" winter	-	3	4	-	5	-	2-4	B
Carrots	2	3-8	3-6	-	-	5-4	6-5	BSL
Celery	2	3	-	4	5	7-3	8-2	BS
Celeriac	2	3	-	-	5	-	9-2	BS
Chards	2	3	4-6	-	4-6	-	9-12	B
Courgettes	3	3-4	5	4	5	5-7	6-9	S
Cucumbers	1-4	2	-	4	-	4-11	-	S
" ridge	3-4	4	-	4	5	-	6-9	S

	Sow	Sow	Sow	Plant	Plant	Harvest	Harvest	BSL
	warm	u/c	o/s	u/c	o/s	u/c	o/s	
Kales	-		3	4	4	4-7	-	9-4	L
Kohlrabi	-		6-8	6-7	6-8	7	-	8-9	B
Leeks	1		2-3	3	-	5-6	-	9	BL
Lettuce	-		2-5	4-7	3-5	5-7	5	6	B
" winter	-		9-10	-	9-11	-	10-1	-	B
Marrow	-		3-4	5	-	5	-	7-9	S
Onion s	1		2	3	3	4	7	8	BS
" Japan	-		-	8	-	-	-	6	-
Onion s	-		-	-	2	3	6	7	BS
Parsnips		-	-	3	-	-	-	12	L
Peas		-	-	3-7	-	-	-	6-9	B
Peppers		2	3	-	4	6	5	8	B
Potatoes		-	-	-	12-3	3-6	4	7-9	S
Pumpkin		3	3	5	4	5	6	7-9	S
Radishes		1	2	3	--	-	3-11	4-10	B
" winter		-	-	7-8	-	-	-	11	S
Shallots sets		-	-	-	-	2-4	-	6-7	S
" seed		-	2-3	3-4	-	3-4	-	7	S
Spinach		1	2-4	3-8	-	-	4-10	5-9	B
" winter		-	8-9	8	-	-	9-3	10-3	B

" N. Zealand	-	-	3	-	-	-	6-10	B
Squashes	3	3	5	4	5	6	7-9	S
Swedes	-	5	5-7	-	6	-	7-3	BS
Sow	Sow	Sow	Plant	Plant	Harvest	Harvest	BSL	
warm	u/c	o/s	u/c	o/s	u/c	o/s		
Sweet corn	3	4-5	4-5	-	5-6	-	7-9	B
Tomatoes	1	2	-	4	5	5-10	7-9	B
Turnips	-	2-3	3-5	4	4-5	4-6	5-9	B

Printed in Poland
by Amazon Fulfillment
Poland Sp. z o.o., Wrocław

50231958R00045